The Child I Was

Autobiography of a Child with Asperger's Syndrome

Manuel Cedeño

Biography of Manuel Cedeño

By Iris Rivero

When autism knocked on my door I had no choice; I had to attend to it... God knows it hasn't been easy, but He has put many people in my way with the desire to help me. Manuel Cedeño has been an immense support and through these letters I want to thank him on my behalf and on behalf of many families for bringing with his testimony a hope for those of us who dream of a better world for our children. THANK YOU!

Today, talking about Manuel Cedeño (@SoyAspie) is a necessary reference when approaching to the world of autism, his successful activism in social networks is given by the fact of narrating in first person his experiences, sufferings, fears, triumphs and failures. He was recently diagnosed with Asperger's Syndrome, a diagnosis that came to answer many of the questions that arose in his day-to-day life.

He is a successful businessman with studies in Economics and Accounting (Andrés Bello Catholic University), a degree in Business Administration (Universidad Nacional Abierta), certified as a Legal Translator of the Bolivarian Republic of Venezuela (Ministry of Interior and Justice), professor at the National School of Human Rights in Caracas, founding president of the @SoyAspie Foundation (@FundAspie), writer, entrepreneur and lecturer. He has a beautiful family, is a father, son and husband. Firstborn of the union between Manuel A. Cedeño and Luisa A. Carpio who from a very young age worked hard to create a family nucleus in which love was the main ingredient. He is a result of a desired pregnancy, his mother was only twenty years old at that time and she remembers many of the emotions of waiting for who would be her first baby. Manuel was born in Maracaibo on May 24, 1970 and would soon become the older brother of Maria Luisa, Livia and David. He was an excessively quiet, lonely, clumsy child, self-absorbed, however he learned to read at a very early age, he was considered an advanced and intelligent student, in fact at the age of 5 he was already enrolled in the first grade, he had to live with the frustration of not knowing or not being able to establish friendly ties with other children, he says that from his earliest age he felt different from others.

During his childhood and adolescence he suffered the most terrible bullying by many of his peers, who used to hate the differences and subjected him to physical, verbal and psychological abuse, details of which today he prefers not to evoke. He is concerned that today bullying continues being part of the school life and what is worse that this happens with the tacit approval of teachers and other students.

The questions that always haunted his mind were answered two years before to be diagnosed for first time, when his nephew (Ramses), then a teenager, was referred for psychological evaluation, later receiving the diagnosis of Asperger's Syndrome. This fact motivated Manuel to investigate what the syndrome was and that was when he realizes that the affectations of the condition were exactly those that he had endured throughout his life, that these characteristics described him perfectly, reason that motivated him to get an evaluation and in 2012 he was diagnosed for first time by Dr. Myriam Ortiz, from that moment he decides to start an activism in social networks for which he creates a campaign under the user @SoyAspie. This campaign aims to disseminate information about autism and raise awareness among parents, teachers, students and the community in general to make a strong rejection of bullying, his humility and selfless love make him able to offer the help and guidance he did not receive as a child, making contributions to prevent further suffering and trauma to children who today live with some diversity. His activism is not limited to the use of social networks but also offers conferences at events related to the above-mentioned topics, making it clear that affectations can be overcome and that this child who was unable to hold a conversation with his peers, is today capable of leading and telling his testimony in auditoriums with hundreds of people.

This is his first book, in which he relates various episodes of his life, affectations and situations in which he was involved as a result of his disability, he says that he was adapting "to the blows" to the surrounding world because although he attended several psychological consultations during his childhood and adolescence, for that time very few specialists were able to diagnose this syndrome, at that time almost unknown, this lack of knowledge generated that some aspies (as people with the condition usually call themselves), were plunged into depression, pain and sadness. Many of them abandoned their studies because of the terrible bullying they received, and many others went until the extreme of attempting to kill themselves.

Without a doubt, the experiences of this man are an example of faith, constancy and courage. His struggle stopped being individual to become collective and prevent other children from continuing to suffer in silence, abandoning their studies and having depressive tendencies that constantly expose their lives. That is why I recommend this book to support you in the dissemination of this information, which helps to detect alerts early, thus promoting a better quality of life for our children.

BEd. Iris Rivero (**@reinadmoros**)

Primary school teacher and mother of an aspie child

From Despair to Hope

By Iris Rivero

What you are about to read changed my view of an adverse circumstance I lived in a moment of my life. Since I was very young I wanted to be a mother. I visualized the future of my children and almost imagined all the history of their life. Maybe it was optimism, maybe illusion, but in my mind my children future was full of successes, loves, and happiness. The long-awaited pregnancy came between one love and another, goals and projects. I was not asked about sex, hair type, skin color, anything... My heart, as a mother, only asked that he be a healthy child. A few months later we knew that we had to think collectively, it was not just one child; it was two... God decided to reward my waiting and my illusion with two children.

Dreaming about them, getting my hopes up, was easy. I just used to close my eyes and different scenarios, and characters appeared before me, and anything was possible in those stories that my mind built on my children. The children were born, and one day, when they were very small, in a cold office I heard the word "AUTISM" and I couldn't dream anymore. I was afraid. Everything was confusing, the doubts were immense, the fear was omnipresent and the despair unbearable. I was wondering why me? Why one of my kids? All those stories faded from my mind, and panic flooded my days. I could not understand how even being a teacher it was so complicated for me everything new that was happening with one of my children, maybe nothing was so new but in those days I could become aware and look for information about that condition that is part of my child. I read a lot, I investigated a lot, but nothing could bring back my faith and the hopes of those stories I dreamed of were more and more distant. So much searching for information overwhelmed me; I didn't have the capacity to read everything and at the same time attend to my child's continuous "tantrums"; now I realized that he was always different.

One day I went to an auditorium and listened to Manuel Cedeño, author of this book, and in that conference, using simple language, he achieved what the multiple contents that I had downloaded into my computer had not achieved, readings that although made me understand theoretically what was going on, none of them were capable of getting me into what my little son was feeling. The fact of knowing his condition in adulthood, immerses Manuel in a life mission that he assumes with humility and commitment. You only have to look at one day of his interactions on social networks (@SoyAspie) to notice the impact of his writings on many families who are in search of hope.

Understanding this disability from the point of view of those who live it, makes our daily work with our children easier. Hence the importance of every anecdote and every writing in first person. That's why I think it's valuable to theoretically understand autism spectrum disorders (ASD) but to get closer to the feelings of the people we love, that's simply essential.

This book also makes it clear that we need to move towards the inclusive society that many of us yearn for. Many times people look at the external behavior of the individual and It Is more important if it is out of tune or annoying, than what that human being is feeling and trying to express, perhaps in a socially incorrect way.

We are alarmed by the world's indifference towards what any child with autism may be feeling while being ignored or misunderstood by peers and adults. Within themselves they carry a battle, some of them exploit and others, like Manuel, become paralyzed and confused. This book encourages you not to ignore to this children. It is an invitation to enter that bubble and give them what they need to be able to express themselves better, and to understand what by their own intuition they cannot understand as others do, and to help them feel self-confidence and love enough to become happy and productive adults.

Preface

This book is part of a three-volume collection dealing with asperger and bullying in first person. The first volume of this trilogy talks about "The Child I Was"; the second is about my experiences as an adult within the autism spectrum, because children with asperger when they grow up don't get cured or die and they still have asperger, and nobody talks about that, how we feel and handle it, but that is the second volume. Finally, the third volume is the author's own essays, opinions and reflections on this subject.

"The Child I Was" is about my childhood as a child with a little-known disability, but not about what the textbooks say about the syndrome, but about how I lived it.

All children with the condition are different and they manifest the asperger in different ways, but because it is not easy to hear a child with autism or asperger's syndrome talk about what he feels and thinks as a direct or indirect effect of his condition or bullying, reading this book can help you understand what it is like for a child to live with asperger's or be a victim of bullying.

This has been expressed to me by people who have read me in more than fifteen countries in Europe, America and Oceania, saying that reading my writings helps them to better understand their children or students, or even themselves in cases where the person reading me has the condition.

The book is recommended for parents of children with autism, so that they know what their children may be feeling, even if they cannot express it; for elementary and secondary school teachers, so that they have an illustrated idea of the warning signs that could help them guide parents in referring children for evaluation for early screening or diagnosis, and for pediatricians, psychologists, psychiatrists, and therapists who want to have an additional idea to what the theory says.

In fact, the book you have in your hands, is not a theoretical book, nor is it based on research, nor scientific studies; here I tell you my testimonies and experiences as a child who being within the autistic spectrum had to suffer and how I had to become strong to survive and learn without any of the tools and support that thank God our children have today.

It is precisely so that all children with this condition have the right support and tools, that I want there to be at least one book like this in every school and in every family in the world, to create awareness and build bridges from what you know today to what will be revealed to you after reading this book.

Manuel Cedeño

To all children on the autism spectrum around the world, to those who are still victims of bullying and to their parents who never tire of struggling.

Then the Lord put forth his hand, and touched my mouth. And the Lord said unto me, Behold, I have put my words in thy mouth.

Jeremiah 1:9

I Mule Driver

My grandfather was a country man, rustic and practical, he had to work too hard to support his wife and the nine children they had together. There's a lot things to do in the country, my grandfather was a mule driver. A mule driver was a trade that existed when there were no lorries or trucks and merchandise was transported from one city to another by mule or ox. The mule driver usually walked but when the merchandise transported was cattle (my grandfather carried cattle) the mule driver travelled on horseback, and in almost all cases accompanied by other mule drivers who helped him herd the beasts. He and his companions always wore hats, canteens and chimps.

One the children that my grandfather had to support

was my father (Manuel), who, like another of my uncles (Maro), had serious problems of socialization, communication, and imagination (my uncle more than my father). Manuel had many things to learn in the countryside, tilling the land, sowing, harvesting, building mud houses, making palm roofs, making cheese, making cassava, or being a mule driver like his father.

However, the imagination of Manuel was so crazy that having so many useful things to learn and do in the country, he wanted to learn English, he didn't tell anyone that, because he wasn't good at communications, but something strange happened in his head that he was studying English obsessively, even though this was absolutely useless.

That's why they say that autistic spectrum people have the imagination affected, because the common people can't understand the things that go through our minds, those crazy ideas, those exits where nobody sees them. But let's go back to the countryside in the mid-20th century:

My grandmother told me that my father used to spend hours studying English. My grandfather, sometimes when he was at home (because he traveled a lot for his job as a mule driver) heard him repeating the phrases and words that he studied in that unintelligible language and said:

Boy, those flounders - and he laughed funny.

But my father did not study like the other children, to provide an examination, but on his own initiative and pleasure, and also in a self-taught way as is common in us. Even if that was useless, even if it was a total waste of time, he did not stop his obsession. Everyone knew that in a town where no one spoke English or was interested in learning it, in a country where no one lived to exploit his knowledge in that language, spending hours and days studying that or any foreign language was a total waste of time and energy, not only because you couldn't live of it, but also because you couldn't even use it to talk to someone else because apart from the fact that it was very difficult for my father to socialize and communicate in Spanish, nobody spoke English in San Fernando de Apure. But he studied English passionately and when an aspie child has an obsession, it's very difficult to get it out of his head.

For the common imagination you have to be brave or crazy to spend hours learning something useless if there are so many useful things to do and learn. Being a mule driver is not so easy as it seems, it has its technique, and it requires practice and takes time, but my dad never learned it, he had no time or interest.

But things change and in retrospect we can see that what one day seemed to be an obsessive, hollow and meaningless interest was in fact somehow the road to self-realization. That obsession, whatever it may be, can lead us to meet people, or learn things that can change the lives of ourselves and others. More than fifty years have passed and my father now lives in his good apartment in Caracas, a city where he could not come as a child or visit because he had no resources. Today, the mule driver profession no longer exists in Venezuela, but there is the Official Translator (Public Interpreter) profession and one of the few ones in the country with a degree in English is my father who lives honestly and comfortably from the legal translation of documents.

That's why my dad is my hero, the warrior that God gave me to show me with his steps the way, and to teach me with his life and his example that even if the world thinks you have to be and think like a mule driver, I'm not crazy for thinking and dreaming of something that "doesn't make sense". Because only those of us who have a different imagination know that what today is not possible, tomorrow can be.

II The Apartment

When we moved to Guarenas I was only four years old, I have many memories of that time, most of them insignificant anecdotes. I remember that I had two beautiful young parents, the former child Manuel who grew up in San Fernando de Apure and his beautiful young wife, Luisa, my mother.

Before we moved to Guarenas we lived in a room that we barely left for the rest of the apartment. I guess my twenty year old mother was sorry that the presence of her two small children all over the house could cause discomfort and that's why we barely left the room.

My dad often talked about buying a house. One day we made a long trip. I remember the exact moment when we arrived, at last... My parents opened the door for the first time to an apartment located on the third and last floor at the end of a long corridor with apartments on the left and a balcony on the right, the balcony facing a parking lot (empty at that time) and another similar building in front. We were three children: my sister Maria Luisa 3 years old, Livia, less than a year old, and me. The apartment was huge, clean and empty. I immediately felt an enormous freedom, I could run freely around the house without bothering anyone. I didn't say anything, but in every corner I shouted vowels that echoed, and to celebrate I got into my small white convertible pedal car and drove around the apartment happy.

My parents were happy too, their two young children and their newborn baby finally had a place to grow up. If I had had the ability to express my feelings I would have run to them and said something. But I didn't talk to them. Instead I drove my white pedal car while my little sister ran around the house and my parents kissed. However, even though I didn't say anything, I was the happiest child in the world.

PS: Most Aspies, especially in the early days of our childhood, have difficulty expressing very great joys. It's not that we don't feel anything, but that we find it difficult to express it. There are therapies, techniques and exercises that can help us to express our feelings and emotions out loud, and the sooner they are started the better.

III The Christmas Tree

Although Guarenas is a hot city, the month of December of the year in which we arrived was cold. At that time, global warming was a science fiction issue and in December temperatures were low to the point that when we spoke, "smoke" used to come out of our mouths.

I was four years old, and due to we came from living in a room where additionally we didn't have a TV, besides the "smoke" that used to come out when we talked, there were another many things that I didn't know yet and that I had never seen. But that didn't make my world simple. It was full of emotions, characters and imaginary situations that I only shared with my sister Maria Luisa and that made it colorful and complex.

Maria Luisa was less than a year younger than me and was the only person with whom I spoke fluently, but even with her I did not share my feelings, which does not mean that I did not have them.

Since it was the first time that our immediate family had its own house and TV, and we were starting to go out for walks, everything was new to me. It was like the world was being created before my eyes.

One of these things I hadn't seen yet was a Christmas tree. One weekend of that December we went out as a family to the park El Trapiche where in the 19th century there was a sugar cane plantation from which there is still a gigantic sugar cane mill as a silent witness of remote times that will not come back. We walked all over the parkDad told us we were looking for the tree. Since my parents had not become professional at that time, we were poor and could not buy one.

I, as literal as I was, imagined a tree like those in the woods but of my own size, and together with Maria Luisa, I ran everywhere looking for it.

Dad finally got a dry stem about mom's height, which was tall for me at the time. I was surprised it was so big because in Spanish Christmas tree is said "arbolito" (small tree).

At home and before the curiosity of the children, mom fixed the stem by burying it in a milk can full of soil inside and wrapped in colored paper outside. She surrounded the can with shoe boxes wrapped in colored paper, and walked back a few steps to see from the best angle how her work was fitting. Maria Luisa and I were happy. Mom came over again and continued working.

The stem rised up beyond Mom's head. She smeared it with white glue and did the same with the branches that came out of it. In the upper part she placed cotton that was adhered with the glue and asked us to do the same with the lower part. We had a world of fun.

Once the tree was dressed entirely in cotton, like snow, Mom, with white sewing thread hung from the branches some little red, yellow and green balls, and bright tears of the same colors in which my sister and I were reflected distorted and upside down, which made us burst out laughing until our bellies hurt.

Soon the dry branch we brought home had turned with my mother's love into a Christmas tree covered with snow and full of magic fruits that turned us upside down. As if that wasn't enough, Mom surrounded it with an extension of colorful lights and placed a red and silver star at the top.

I was ecstatic about that magic tree that Mom had made from a simple dry branch that Dad gave her.

—That's love," she said, without my asking. She was one of those mothers who hears thoughts and sometimes doesn't need words. She added, —Love turns the ugly and dry into something beautiful—.

My heart wrinkled because it foresaw that I would never live a moment like that again.

Forty years have passed since that December. I now frequent the most modern shopping malls in the country, and I've seen there Christmas trees of all colors and sizes. I even saw one the size of a four-story building adorned with swarovski stones worth a fortune; but, I've never seen one more beautiful than that dried up branch that Mom transformed with her magic at Christmas.

IV Lost

One of my readers tells me that she wants to send her 12-year-old aspie boy alone on a bus or in a taxi somewhere, but that she's afraid because she doesn't know how Asperger affects the action of locating and moving around. She asks me if my mom did send me alone on a bus or in a taxi somewhere at that age and what I think about it.

It is good to comment that it is not rare that the sense of orientation, as well as the threshold of pain, the rhythm of speech, the recognition of faces, among others, are altered in the Conditions of the Autism Spectrum, however contrary to other conditions such alteration is not always in the same direction, but it can be in different people towards different extremes, that is to say from almost the absence of it in some people to the extremely sensitive and sophisticated in others.

My personal case. Spatial orientation:

I particularly have the sense of spatial location extremely affected towards the negative end. In other words, my sense of direction is far below that of the average person, so I'll tell you some anecdotes:

Our new apartment was in a building that had in the ground floor a parking lot with a single exit to the street, to the left (leaving from my building), or to the right leaving from the building in front. When I was five years old, a blue station wagon used to drive into my neighborhood, parked and shouted through a megaphone:

— The baker's here, the baker's here. — There were no bakeries nearby yet.

To get to my apartment, you had to go up the stairs to the top floor (those three-story buildings didn't have elevators) and walk down a straight hallway from where you could see the parking lot, the building in front of it, and the street. I lived in the last apartment in that hallway.

When the baker came, my mom sometimes sent me to buy it. From the entrance of my apartment and along the hallway you could see the station wagon downstairs, my mom used to give me some coins and I went downstairs to buy the bread.

After I paid, I realized that the two buildings in front and behind me were identical. Its stairs and hallways with apartments were identical, both had three floors, the same structure, the same color... but which one of them did I live in? Now I realize that the solution was very easy, because my building was the one behind me if I walked without turning. But at the time, for some reason I couldn't tell if I was coming from behind or from the front. The chance of getting it right was 50-50, after all if I made a mistake I only had to go down the stairs and up the ones in the building opposite, which was certainly correct one, there was no a third option.

I never went up the three floors of the other building, I always heard my mom screaming in the distance:

—It's not there, it's here, hey here. — Even though I hardly had to walk, just go down and up, she kept an eye on me.

I also remember that when I was walking on a sidewalk in front of my parents, for example towards the north and we crossed the street, to follow the path but on the other sidewalk, when I crossed I no longer knew which way to go, now I know that the logical thing was to follow the same direction (in this case towards the north), the problem was that when I turned to cross the street I was already disoriented and did not know if I was coming from there or from here and therefore where to go. One day when I was seven years old, after crossing the street I asked where to go, my father told my mother that I had no sense of direction, at that moment I became aware of this affectation and in silence I proposed not to get lost when crossing the street and to maintain my awareness of the direction in which I was walking, this I achieved, at least in the act of crossing the street.

At the age of nine, after five years of coming and going every day to school with a neighbor that my mom and several mothers hired to take their children to and from school (like transportation but on foot), I already knew the way by heart, and my mom tried to send me there alone. I walked up and down without any problems the route of my whole life. My mom did well in giving me that vote of confidence that generated in me security and self-esteem.

Once, when I was 21 years old, walking with a group from the university, I saw in Altamira (Caracas) a place called "El Muro" or something like that. We didn't go in but I liked the decoration of the facade and it seemed appropriate for me to take my girlfriend (current wife) to listen to music, have a drink and talk. Days later I invited her. We walked for hours, I never got the place. Even when we were dating, we got lost in a trip to the river and were almost surprised by the night in the middle of the mountain. (My wife says that with all those signs she refused to see what I was like. That's why they say that love is blind).

When I bought my first car, at the age of 27, I used to park it and spent hours looking for it because I couldn't find the place where I parked, then I devised a technique by writing down the parking space with all the possible references.

I still get disoriented nowadays. The malls I often visit are two, one in front of the other, many times I don't know if I am in one or the other, I doubt sometimes where I parked and I often have to turn around. To look for a place, even if I've been there several times, I systematically go through the whole mall, aisle by aisle and level by level until I find it.

Almost always, with the exception of weekends, I move with a driver or with my wife, even when I go to a place I already know. I prefer my driver to drive, largely because of the orientation issue that causes me a lot of anxiety and tension while driving unless it is a route already learned by heart. When for some reason I drive and go alone in the car, if it is not towards a place I frequent, I use GPS, otherwise I suffer a lot. My wife memorizes the roads and routes by going only once and also finds other routes by deducting them I don't know how. She has a fabulous sense of direction, and that makes up to me. For example, I can go alone to many places in the city where I live (Guatire), also to my office (in Caracas), my mother's house, and many places that I know by heart because I have been going there for many years. But if it's a place where I' ve been going less than ten times, I can get there, but after a lot of driving around, asking questions and suffering a lot.

Once four years ago I was driving with my mom in my car and she, maybe a little uncomfortable because of my disorientation, told me that I shouldn't drive (we didn't know about the asperger yet). She told me this in a good way, but in that moment it hurt me, I did not understand her in her right dimension and I wrote her an email (almost always when I really communicate I do it in writing) asking her never again to tell me that I cannot do something, that I am capable of doing and learning all things. But now looking at it from here, with the knowledge I now have about the syndrome that affects me, and considering that she knows me since my birth, I understand her concern.

Other cases. Spatial orientation.

Now, on this subject my case could be considered extreme, in spite of this I have progressed and I know that with exercises and some kind of therapy I can improve more and more, so don't be alarmed. On the other hand as I told you above there are people with Asperger's syndrome who have a super-developed sense of direction, I share with you experiences of other people to see how different we can be:

— My mom, who has raised my 14-year-old nephew with Asperger's Syndrome for most of his life, says he has a very poor sense of direction. My nephew already knows how to go to his high school alone although my mother, like all grandmothers, overprotects him and prefers him to go with her or on the transport.

— My brother, who may have undiagnosed Asperger's syndrome, has a bad sense of direction. My mom, even before she knew about the syndrome, always said that he shouldn't drive because of his disorientation and sudden movements at the wheel.

-My daughter, although she doesn't have Asperger's Syndrome (at least as far as I know), is affected by her sense of spatial orientation at almost the same level as mine.

-Fátima Matiuda, from Paraguay, a woman with Asperger graduated in law, tells me: "I have a photographic memory for points of reference and my sense of orientation is extraordinarily developed, it's as if I had a map and coordinates in my head"

— Once I went to one of the support groups organized by the Fundasperven Foundation, one of the kids with Asperger's Syndrome (twenty-five years old) who was sitting next to me and his mother got up, went to the bathroom and on the way back he got lost. His mother and I saw him about three hundred meters away lost in the grass, hesitating and looking all over. He finally spotted us. The same thing happends to me in that place. I always get lost.

Maria Añangure wrote from Caracas:

"Oh, Manuel I identify with you. I also lack a sense of direction, so I don't like to go out alone and when I take a shortcut I get short of breath because of how I feel. I, like you, get to places by reference points, so I ask for a known and easy to locate reference point. I was recently going to meet a friend to pick up a shipment on the Av. Panteón. I get to the site and find out it's closed. Since I don't have a cell phone, I had to walk two blocks to find a public phone. When I finished the call I looked at the place and as it was not known to me, my heart began to beat wildly, and I began to sweat cold. It was horrible. I finally got over it and arrived at a street I know, but seen from another angle it looks different. The shock clouded my vision. It was seconds but as I was saturated trying to locate myself I didn't realize I knew the street. Anyway, I arrived at my destination not without suffering for getting lost. It still happens to me that when I cross a street that I hadn't planned on, I get disoriented, but then I get situated.

Rebekah Pino wrote from Caracas:

"My daughter has a photographic memory. When she was about four years old we went to her grandmother's house, I was lost and she said: Mommy, this is where my grandmother lives." And indeed we came out right in front of Grandma's house, I hadn't noticed. I was very surprised."

Ayaris García(@ayarigarcia2108) wrote from Cagua, Aragua, Venezuela:

"You made me laugh with the story of your mom screaming "not there". I do the same with my beautiful nine-year-old aspie. When he passed to the third grade he was moved to another school building and it took almost two months for him to memorize where he should go now. I stayed hidden because he asked me to leave him alone, I suffered seeing him stop to remember where he had to go, if it took too long I ran to help him and of course he didn't like that. He memorizes the places where we park and the colors of the doors, establishments nearby, but I'm sure that if for some reason that varies, he would get lost and that worries me but I'm already working on finding a solution, because also when he's not attentive but immersed in one of his continuous internal talks, he doesn't know where I'm taking him."

Sandra Olivares wrote from Mexico:

That area has cost us a lot of work... and it's still in process.

Luis Mejías Sarmiento wrote from Caracas:

"hahahahaha thanks Manuel, you just cleared up one of the biggest doubts of my life. I've always been more lost than Adam on Mother's Day. I've gotten lost in Caracas, in Miami, in Europe, in parking lots and almost anywhere, thanks to the smart phones I take pictures of the closest places to be able to locate myself, there are cases that I have to use a GPS"

Ingrid Georgina Can wrote from Mexico:

"My son has an impressive memory if we go to a square and come back six months later he remembers perfectly where everything is. Greetings."

Alejandro Castro Ulloa (@acastroulloa) wrote from Colombia:

"When I was very young, I was enrolled in a gigantic school. When we returned from the break it was a torment for me because I always got lost. I couldn't find the classroom and I got into the wrong ones (I didn't even recognize the kids of my class); the anguish was terrible, my parents had to move me to another school".

"Viajes Destinos" wrote:

"Manuel, my eight-year-old son has an incredible memory for remembering places".

V Monsters in the Darkness

In the middle of the darkness, the light from the street-lamp at the entrance to the car park lit up the ceiling of my bedroom. The beam of light split as it hit the slats of the jalousie window and entered my bedroom in a broken pattern, forming stairs of white light on the ceiling.

The stairs did not stand still, but rather moved when the beam flickered on and off or they were distorted as the beam was interrupted or affected by the headlights of some car entering or leaving the car park of the building.

It was just white light on my ceiling, but it seemed as if it came to life in the middle of the dark night, and its reflection allowed me to see the Gothic ornament on the small door to the chiffonier in front of my bed.

The ornament was an abstract figure consisting of two branches full of leaves; the arched branches formed a circle between them, within which there were also small leaves. All this was made of raised wood, brown in colour like the chiffonier, but darker.

Such branches —that the little four-year-old boy was staring at as much as the little light entering the room allowed him, — seemed suddenly to vanish and appear, perhaps because of the effect of light or sleep.

The little boy gently tapped the blue wall (which at that time looked black) with his fingertips with taps spaced at equal intervals, thus making a rhythmic sound; perhaps to break the silence, perhaps to feel that he had some power, the power to make some sound, but power anyway.

Suddenly, the leaves of the chiffonier's Gothic ornament moved at the same rhythm as the tapping on the wall. What? Is this possible? No! But it happened. I'd better relax and watch more carefully. A car is entering, the stairs play their game, the tapping sound continues and... I think the leaves moved again... That leaf is moving right now! Oh, my God! It has disappeared, plunged into the darkness. Could a little creature be hiding behind the chiffonier door? No, it can't be! But I stopped tapping the wall, and someone else tapped it again!

Something is going on here, and I'm scared. My room is in darkness and I am alone in here… but I am sure I'm not alone, there is a strange presence here. The stairs move without any car coming in, the Gothic figure disappears for a few seconds and I have to blink several times to make it appear again. I think I'm going to tell my dad and see if he will protect me, I'm really scared.

When I'm about to get up I think of some living creatures that, like the monsters in the darkness, are here in my room, all together playing a bad joke on me; these horrible creatures come out at night; they are brown creeping insects, with useless brown wings and big black eyes like oval spots; they are revolting... and terrify me. Just, when I'm about to get up to look for my dad, I stop abruptly before putting my feet on the cold floor to get my slippers.

No, I can't do it! There must be a cockroach there, next to my slippers, with its big black spots for eyes, its disgusting antennae and its useless wings, down there waiting for me to climb up on my feet as soon as they touch the floor. I can't do this!

The stairs keep moving, even though no car is passing now; someone tapped the wall slightly, I am almost sure, I heard it and the Gothic figure on the chiffonier has turned into the face of an old man with a mocking smile.

I can't stand it any longer! It's now or never! I jump on the floor and look for my slippers… luckily I find them before a cockroach finds me, and I go to the next bedroom where my beautiful young parents are sleeping.

I can't talk yet, although I can read. I don't know how to explain to my dad all the things that are happening right now in the next bedroom, but I can say a few words, so I wake him up with a touch:

"Dad, I'm scared." That's all I can say.

Dad gets up; maybe he is sleepy, but he is tall and strong, and I know that the monsters in the darkness will not withstand his presence.

Indeed, we enter the room, without turning on the light, and the room is peaceful: The stair of light moves only if a car enters or leaves, nobody is tapping the wall and the Gothic figure has returned to the chiffonier door, the old mocking man is not there any more.

Now I can close my eyes and relax, because I know there is no real or imaginary monster that would dare to touch me if Dad is around... Zzzzz

VI The Recess

My First Day of School

When, on my first day of school, the bell rang announcing the start of recess and my teacher Juanita said we could go outside for recess, the children came out of the classroom in droves, and some of them walked through the door almost at the same time bumping into each other. I thought then that I was not in the right place, why are they in such a hurry? Where are they going? Why do they scream and talk so much and so hard? The confusion, the doubts, the anxiety invaded me but I didn't want them to think that I was weird. I had the feeling that I had missed something or that the other children had agreed to go out together without my noticing, but when, why didn't I notice?

I decided to go out and pretend I was just like all the other children but I walked slowly for fear of tripping or falling. I wanted to become invisible and I think in a way I succeeded because when I got to the playground a kid passed me running and screaming and almost knocked me down but I didn't fall. Although annoyed by the incident I was tolerant and kept walking quietly.

I saw many faces, all laughing or screaming. I could not recognize anyone, they all looked the same to me, this happened to me for a long time until after several months I started to fix in my mind a few faces. But especially that first day, the noise and shouting stunned me and made it even more confusing that I had no idea what to do at that moment. A ball buzzed through the air and in its flight it seemed to go towards me and endanger my physical integrity. I noticed that everyone, absolutely every child except me seemed to be playing, having fun, or at least chatting excitedly.

But I decided to be brave: -if I don't do what they do, they'll think there's something wrong with me. I will go to a group and act like them.

And I tried, I swear I tried, but that day I couldn't even get near the other kids. There I stood at recess, alone and moving my right arm and hand up and down rhythmically, with my feet nailed to the floor and unable to move or speak.

The bell rang to mark the end of the recess and released me from that kind of trance. I returned to my classroom after peeking at several of them until I recognized my teacher. I was relieved that it was over, but I hated myself for not being able to overcome the isolation that I felt for the first time and that although I didn't know it then, I couldn't understand, overcome or break it until many years later.

The Worst Time in School

For children with a typical neurobiological condition, recess is the best time in school, it is the opportunity to compete, to play, to talk, etc. For me it was instead the worst time at school, I didn't know what to do, where to go or how to act and that can be deeply stressful, and if you don't have a good help it can seriously hurt the child's self-esteem and school performance.

When I speak of good help I refer to good communication with parents, the support of a teacher who is aware of the Asperger's syndrome, the intervention of his psychiatrist or therapists and even, if possible, the participation of a support group for the child made up of some classmates who are educated about the condition and who want to collaborate in his/her inclusion and in learning the implicit codes of behavior that we cannot perceive intuitively. These support groups can be very productive, protect the child from possible bullying, and could develop into real and lasting friendships over time.

One of the reasons why recess was such a hard time for me, is because unlike classes in the classroom where everything is structured and the rules are clear, at recess it doesn't happen that way. When I was in school, during class it was easy to know what to do: read, do the math, find the diphthongs, write the prime numbers, divide into syllables, take dictation, etc. Things were clear in class, but at recess all the children seemed to have a secret code that let them know exactly what to do, how and what to play, where to go, etc. Everything seemed perfectly clear to the kids who were literally running to play their roles... except for me.

—Should I stay in my seat reading after I eat my snack, or should I go out and play? If I stay here reading I'm going to look very strange, and they'll want to bother me, but if I go out, where do I go? And if I play, with whom and what? When the children hit the ball they run and I don't know why or where. Besides, I've already tried and I can't hit the ball in the air, they'll laugh and say bad things to me...

I used to go out quietly and alone, wandering the courtyards and corridors, discreetly studying the other children. I remember that until I was six years old, while I was walking around the courtyards analyzing the other children, I used to execute a stereotype with my right hand and arm, moving them in a circular motion, back and forth. Now I know that this stereotype made me seem even more strange and decreased the possibility of anyone approaching me. It is important that parents work to make their children aware of the convenience of shaping, controlling or eliminating some of these strange movements or behaviors, in order to facilitate socialization and inclusion.

Several times I approached the children to wait for a turn to play. My heart was racing with stress waiting for the moment, and when it was my turn, I couldn't play and only caused laughter. This kind of reaction from my peers made me afraid to participate in the games, so my strategy became to delay the snack as much as possible and then go out to study the social behavior of the other children, always with the danger of being bullied for not being equal to them.

It is for this reason that I write this book, because I know that with directed recreation strategies and the support and constant vigilance of the parents through a strong bond of communication between the child, his teachers and his parents; and with conscientious, allied and respectful teachers and classmates, the recess bell will no longer freeze anyone's blood, and those minutes will be what they are meant to be: a time of healthy leisure and recreation.

VII Hyperlexia

Although a minority of people with high-functioning Autism or Asperger's syndrome have difficulty learning to read, the vast majority have some degree of hyperlexia. It is mainly characterized by learning to read at a much earlier age than the average. This learning also occurs naturally or spontaneously, that is to say without pressure, effort or even intention from other people, and there are cases of children who learn to read even at the age of two.

I have saved somewhere a drawing that my brother David made for me when we were children. It is a teddy bear and has my name and the date written in his handwriting. When he gave it to me it seemed natural but after checking my things as an adult, I see the teddy bear and for my surprise I realize from the dedication dated, that by the time he gave it to me, my brother had just turned three years old.

I don't remember when I learned to read, or how I did it. My dad says that just like my brother David, I learned on my own. What I do remember is that when I was five years old and started my first grade of elementary school, I was already reading fluently. I remember it well because of the impression I got from the fact that kids much older than me (when you're five, two years older is half your life) were studying with me, and they were barely learning to read. That really impressed me, and made me realize for the first time that I was different from the other children. It was the first time I was aware of it. At first, because they were older than me, I assumed that they would read better than me, and that they had read more than me. But I realized that instead they were struggling to understand what was natural and intuitive to me. There was a palpable effort by the children to learn (some of them because others weren't even interested), also an effort by my teacher Juanita Garcia because they learned. I thought:

—How those big children don't understand something so easy? —

But just as reading was intuitive and natural to me and not to them, there were also things that were natural to them and that seemed like a gigantic mystery to me, such as the art of initiating a conversation. This was something I could not do, and if another child initiated it, I did not know how to continue it fluently, I could only say:

—Yes, I do

—No, I don´t.

—Good, thaks.

And so I answered sparingly and concretely or repeated the last sentence I heard.

But this did not happen to me for lack of vocabulary, on the contrary, at the age of six my grandmother Juana gave me a rustic Bible, it had a thick black cover and red borders, it was the Reina Valera 60 version, my first book after the first and second grade school books. For those who do not know it, Reina Valera 60 Bible has an antique language that makes it more difficult to understand, even for an adult. But this did not deter me, when I read a word that I did not know, I looked it up in the dictionary and learned how to use it. At the age of seven I started reading the self-taught encyclopedias that my father had in his library, in which I read about dinosaurs, languages, world history, and many other things. At eleven, while my neighbors played ball on the ground floor of the building where we lived, I read contemporary and classical literature, at fourteen I read Cervantes, in short, I loved reading, which gave me a richer vocabulary than my peers.

All this made the adults believe that I was simply a very intelligent child. But be careful, it's not necessarily always so. People with Asperger's syndrome usually have an IQ that is equal to the average, sometimes higher, which makes it difficult to diagnose because it makes people think that the child does not have special needs. But the fact of learning to read before the average age is not a sign of intelligence, it is rather if it is added to other symptoms, a warning sign that indicates that the child needs to be evaluated by a specialist to determine if there is any special condition or at least areas to be attended to.

It's easy to think that learning to read at such a young age is good, and to believe that when I was "ahead" compared to my classmates I should have thought I was the best. But it's not so. There is nothing great about being able to read if you cannot share what you read with anyone, if you cannot look anyone in the eye, if you cannot converse with the other children. It's not worth reading all the books in the world if you don't have a friend to share them with. In fact, the vocabulary I acquired as a child from reading, the structures of language and grammar, and even the very knowledge of man and society that I gained from reading, were useless to me in practical life, when it came to sitting down with another child to have a natural conversation.

Teacher, mother, father, you have to be aware that that child who seems to be very intelligent, and perhaps is, can be at the same time a child who needs help in areas of development that for the rest of the children are spontaneous. Educate yourself and do not fail to attend to his special needs, if he has them. Because all the letters in the world and all the books on the planet cannot replace the love and support you can give him.

VIII Children Playing

The recess bell rings

I'm scared.

Shall I go out?

No, I'd better stay here reading.

Several children go out at once

They bump and push each other,

But they're happy, they laugh

Why are they leaving in such a hurry?

Where will they go?

I'm stealthily following them

They play something, I don't understand what

I stand back and watch them

I want to have friends

I'm approaching

I sketch a smile

I pretend the game is funny to me

I look invisible

The sun on the asphalt glows

I say it, no one listens to me

Everybody talks at once

They scream; they shout, they stun

A child asks me: do you want to play?

The world is getting smaller for me

I say yes, I get the ball

I don't know what to do with it.

It's rough and dirty

I hear screaming,

they gesture to me with their faces, with their
hands

What do they want?

Bat the ball! They're yelling at me

I throw the ball, it seems that it is urgent

I hear laughter, someone pushes me

He tells me an insult

I let the offense go

I don't want to fight today

I pretend to retire, but I know I've been dumped

I'm going into a corner

I remain silent

I take out an imaginary toy

I get lost in my thoughts

My silence says many things

The breeze takes them away

Adults don't understand these things.

IX Small Lies

There's a myth that children with autism spectrum conditions don't lie. That's not true. I have never been a liar, I do not tell lies for pleasure or as a habit, but to say that I have never told a lie in my life is to tell a lie. It's not something I'm proud of, but this is the truth.

I remember the first lie I told, at least as far as I can remember. I was five years old, I had already put on my yellow pyjamas with white cuffs, they were made of a very soft fabric that gave me a good feeling to the touch, very fresh. Mom had already put me to bed and while I was in bed I started thinking about school. I was annoyed to have to go to school the next day. I was in first grade and going to spend half the day watching my teacher struggling to get the kids to understand how written syllables were pronounced didn't excite me, besides it increased my anxiety to think about recess time and all that it implied for me and not knowing whether or not I got physical education that day.

Then I had a brilliant idea: I'd say I felt bad. Got it! I'll say I have a headache. I stood up, I looked for

Mom and I said, "I have a headache." She immediately took me back to bed, felt my temperature by placing the back of her hand on my neck, put a thermometer on me and left me alone in the room for a moment.

"What a mess I got myself into," I thought, "Mom's going to know that I'm not in any pain when she sees the thermometer measurement, then I'll have to go to school and she's going to know that I lied to her, what did I do! I had another idea to cover up the charade. I took the thermometer out of my mouth, stood on the bed that was against the wall that had the yellow incandescent bulb that lit up my room, and held the thermometer near to the light bulb.

It was distressing seconds. I did not want to let the thermometer raise the temperature too much so that my mom would not think that the matter was serious and she would take me to the hospital «If they take me to the hospital, they'll inject me. No, please!» But I also didn't want to take the thermometer out of the light so fast that the mercury wouldn't react, so I was calculating how many seconds I should stand there with my arm raised and the thermometer near the bulb so it wouldn't be too much or too little time.

But there was also the risk that my mom would come into the room and find me standing on the bed with my arm raised with the thermometer exposed to the light bulb.

I couldn't decide how many seconds I should stay there. I heard Mom's footsteps and saw her come in through the door, but just a second before her figure appeared I jumped into bed, tucked myself in as she left me and put the thermometer in my mouth trying, without much success, to regulate my accelerated breathing.

"What's wrong with you?" Mom asked me. Maybe she noticed me getting agitated. "Nothing" I said without saying a word, shaking my head, scared and in expectation of what the thermometer would read and the consequences it would bring. Mom took it out of my mouth, looked at the line of mercury carefully. I tried to scrutinize her face but I couldn't make out anything, she didn't say anything either, she left the room and left me with my thoughts: «Don't let her come back with an injection machine! Oh God, don't let her take me to the hospital!»

Mom came back with a Bayer children's aspirin, the kind that was tiny and pink. «¿ What will happen to me if I take this aspirin without being sick? Will it make me sick? What if I die? I only wanted to skip school tomorrow, and now I'm in danger of dying». But there was nothing left to do, Mom crushed the aspirin into a small spoon and gave it to me with a little water. I swallowed the aspirin in fear: "My God, please don't let anything happen to me!"».

I fell asleep thinking about this.

The next day Mom asked me how I was feeling and I didn't hesitate to tell her that I was fine. I don't know if it's because of the unpleasant experience, because of my personality or because of why, but I don't remember telling another lie for many years.

With this anecdote I want to make it clear that although we do not usually tell lies, we can do it and most of us have told them at some time or period in our lives. We're bad at lying, we're uncomfortable, and we tend to tell the truth even when it hurts. However, it is an exaggeration to say that someone cannot lie because he or she has autism; that is definitely a myth based on the exaggeration of our characteristics.

X Boy or girl?

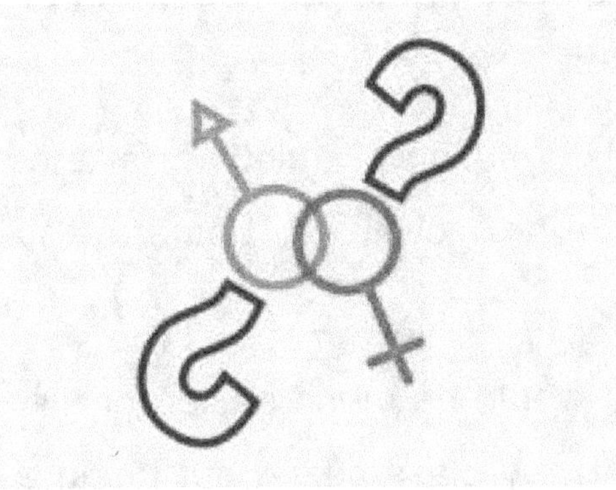

That same year that I started the first grade of primary school, when I was at school, especially at recess, I was tormented by some thoughts. Males used to leave the classroom in a stampede, females were calmer and went out in small groups in a more orderly way. I was one of the last to go out, after the girls and the boys. Just this was enough to give me a strange appearance.

Outside at recess I used to see my peers running up little dirt hills in a large schoolyard and then hurling themselves in pairs from above, rolling over and hitting each other. Others use to do the "pylon", that is, all the children physically fell on top of each other and the ones up hit the ones on the inside the pylon, they screamed, beat each other up and played ball. I watched it in terror,

—You're supposed to do that. —I said to myself, and I went over there smiling and trying to somehow play the less aggressive games. But I went unnoticed most of the time, almost invisible, and that somehow relieved me, but at the same time it made me doubt myself.

I saw the girls, walking quietly, talking, laughing or playing more civilized games and thought:

—If I were a girl it would be much easier for me, I could maybe play with my classmates, but being a boy it is difficult to get close to girls and with boys I cannot play because I am not like them, I cannot do what they do.

Then I concluded:

—I should have been a girl.

That feeling, in my case, was not caused by sexual attraction to the boys but by the frustration of not being able to play their games and not understanding the grace of their jokes and that fact led me to that wrong and delicate conclusion.

At the age of six I realized that I shouldn't have been female because I liked a little girl who always cared about me and defended me from bullying,

— She' s an angel.

I realized that I did not feel this way about any boy, or anyone, she was the most beautiful girl in the world and the most beautiful creature on earth.

In my case I had that angel (I don't remember her name) but she was white with curls and black eyes, a real angel and immediately dispelled my misguided thoughts about my sexuality, but what about the children who don't find an angel like her and get caught up in a thought of sexual identity confusion, like the ones I had? This is not a small thing, children like the one I was need guidance, I had God with me, the only one I could talk to, but we cannot leave everything to God.

What about the children who today, for the wrong reasons, as I did, think:

—There's something wrong with my sexuality because I'm not like other boys. I have a problem. I must have been a girl.

It is important that they have the guidance of parents and therapists who make the child understand that there is nothing wrong with his sexuality or way of being. That there are many boys who are not like those children he knows. There is nothing wrong with being like him and on the contrary he is like precious stones which are something very difficult to get but at the same time something very very precious.

XI Stereotypies

In my first two years at school, at recess, I often turned an imaginary gun three times with my index finger and then abruptly stopped it by pointing it with my forearm perpendicular to the arm and holding the gun tightly. I think I learned how to be so skilled with a gun in one of those black-and-white cowboy movies, or something like that.

Why did I do it? I don't know. Maybe a way to break the glass that I felt was separating me from the world, maybe so that someone would see me and take notice of me, or to seem bold and fearless like the characters in the movies, or because it relaxed me, or maybe all the previous ones, anyway. I executed this movement almost compulsively at recess when all my little friends ate together, ran, played ball, and made groups to fight and play while I watched them close up but far away at the same time. I want to make it clear that I wasn't upset and I certainly didn't want to shoot anyone, I just used to execute the movement.

When I discovered asperger I knew that many aspies execute or executed some kind of repetitive movement at some time in their lives. Then I found an explanation for that behavior and many others. Everything began to fit together.

I clearly remember one day while I was performing my stereotypy alone at recess, I heard two kids a little older than me saying

-Look, he's crazy.

And then they laughed as they pointed at me with total indiscretion.

It was cruel what those children did, but what doesn't kill makes you stronger, and there is a good side to everything. At that moment I realized that this was not "normal" and although I continued walking with my gun in motion so that they would think that I was not affected by their mockery, when I no longer had them in sight I dropped the gun and never took it again.

That cruel cure didn't traumatize me, didn't mutilate me, didn't kill me. I had to find another way to drain all this. Surely that was not the best way to make me aware that that stereotypy was not convenient, but the behavior of those children made me react and eliminate an inconvenient behavior.

There are some behaviors that your child should change or eliminate not because they harm anyone but simply because they harm his or her successful development. There is no one better than you to tell it him/her, don't be afraid, better you do it and don't wait for two cruel children to let him/her know. It hurts less.

XII Flying Ants

May 1976, in a few days I would be six years old. I was finishing the first grade, it was already seven o'clock at night, it was raining heavily. The black and white TV was transmitting I don't know what, I couldn't concentrate on the programming or anything. Mom didn't arrive, and even though I didn't say anything, some questions haunted my head:

—Will she never come back? Will she leave me and my sisters stranded with Grandma María? Did something bad happen to her?

The next day I had classes. From now on, surely, grandma would help me dress instead of mom, it would be grandma who would tuck my khaki shirt of the uniform into my pants and tie my black polished shoes. But it wasn't just a question of who would help me dress. I wanted to see Mom!

The rain sounded beautiful hitting the balcony awning hard. I sat down at the wooden round table and like other times I was fascinated by the light bulb on the balcony wall. Seeing the light directly took away my sleep and my sister and I felt that it gave us strength, besides it made me see very funny colored spots that moved as I moved my eyes; but what fascinated me most about the light in those days was that a swarm of flying ants was dancing around it.

—Where are they the rest of the year, why do they like the light too, do they see coloured spots like me, why do they have wings, what a great privilege they have!

If I were an ant I would be a special ant like them because they live in an incredible, immense and exciting world that the rest of the ants cannot understand or imagine exists. I think something similar is happening to me. What happens to flying ants in relation to other ants must be like what happens to me with my classmates. They, and even the adults, think I'm stupid because I can't talk or play like the other kids, that my head is empty because I don't say anything. They can' t imagine all I know, all I dream, all I think. They don't know me! But just like those ants with respect to their wingless companions, I know things they don't know, let them think what they want!

A thunderclap takes me out of my thoughts. The rain is getting harder, a dog is barking in the distance, is he getting wet? Eight o'clock at night, bedtime according to my routine, and mommy doesn't arrive.

—God make my mom arrive now!

—Go to bed, it's late," says Grandma Maria. My sisters are going to bed. I can't. I'm too anxious.

It thunders. Mommy didn't come. Dad won't be home until tomorrow because he's some kind of doctor who does X-rays in a hospital and is on call today. Grandma sends me to bed again but I don't want to, it scares me, I don't know what can happen if mom isn't home.

The ants are doing a dance that I don't understand. They land, take a few steps, fly in a circle around the light and land again. I approach to observe them better, their wings are transparent. A flash of lightning lights up the sky, one, two, three seconds and something explodes in the sky.

—God make sure nothing happens to Mom.

I hear some keys, my heart skips a beat. Finally she opens the door and walks in soaking wet. She's the most beautiful woman in the world. I ask for her blessing, but I don't give her a hug, nothing. Just like before she arrived I look indifferent, silent, abstracted. I don't talk, I don't smile, I don't ask for anything, I don't tell her about Grillo, the child who bothers me at school and that I have to face again the next day. Nothing. I just stay silent and go back to studying the light and the behavior of the flying ants.

— Go to bed, it's after eight. — She says to me.

— I've already sent him to bed, but he won't listen. Grandma defends herself.

I don't have all the answers, I don't know why there are ants that have wings and ants that don't. I also don't know why they look for the light and do that ritual around it, but I know Mom is home and I'm going to bed happy.

XIII Stereotypies

The apartm   ent we moved into had a large living-dining room that opened onto a long, straight corridor around which the other rooms were distributed. And even though we were already more than three years there and the corridor was straight, that didn't stop me and some of my brothers, walking down it, and suddenly bumping into the walls, preferably hitting the edge with our foreheads: poof! Oops. That happened to us until I was about seven years old. David, my younger brother, didn't hit the walls, but until about he was one year and a half, while he was sitting on the floor, he threw himself back (or fell) hard, hitting the floor with the back of his head, I don't know if he was use to do it intentionally or if he just lost his balance. He even when he was 5 years old walking down that same corridor without tripping over anything used to fall, which is why I used to tell him:

—Be careful you fall!

Warning that many times it was fulfilled as a prophecy.

Are these wall bumps and movements a strange thing? apparently not in a family of high-functioning autistics. In my case I felt like Koji Kabuto driving Massinger Z. When I was eight years old, I wore orthopedic boots with thick steel cables rubberized from the waist to the ankles that helped me walk without turning my feet inward and preventing me from tripping over one foot.

This difficulty in coordinating movements accurately made me suffer a lot in physical education in my school years when it came to catching or hitting a ball, and then as a teenager when it came to learning to dance. Fortunately, at that time, the "merengue" of the '80s was growing rapidly in popularity and was danced carelessly without the need of precise and coordinated movements, unlike "salsa", whose dance technique I could never understand. Merengue and what was then called "miúsik" didn't have this problem, so one could move freely following the rhythm approximately, I, for my part, tried to do it as if nobody was watching me and I enjoyed it.

As a young adult, from the first night we were married, my wife noticed in her own flesh this clumsiness of movement. The brave girl received elbows and knees for my lack of precision or delicacy in coordinating movements, but she was patient. Love helps and experience teaches.

By now, as an adult, I don't bump into walls or fall to the floor, nor do my siblings, but I know an adult with asperger that keeps falling to the floor. I learned to handle the "robot" quite well, although I still feel very much my clumsiness especially for fine motor skills, like writing, untying knots (I suffer when my wife ties several long cables together and making them shorter, because I have a hard time finding the development of the knot), I still have a hard time catching things in the air, the signature on the cheks is rejected because it never comes out the same and in general I have a hard time doing manual works. When I'm in that position, I make an effort to prevent others from noticing my suffering, and I think that's more counterproductive, so I avoid making movements and works that reveal my clumsiness.

It is only now in the 21st century, many years later, that I learned that what I have described here is part of the afflictions of a syndrome called asperger's, and it's only now that all these things, inexplicable until recently, have found an answer. Now I understand that it's not just me and my brothers. I now know an adult asperger girl who tells me that even today at this age she still stumbles over the walls.

Natacha, my sister-in-law with severe autism and moderate cognitive impairment is now an adult, but she still stumbles over walls, streetlights, and falls to the floor from time to time, but she has a tougher condition than I do. We high-functioning aspergers or autistic people have a lot of potential to improve our motor skills. I, on the other hand, do very well in my environment and with the activities I chose to earn my living, so you, if you are asperger, I assure you that you can greatly improve your fine or gross motor coordination, and be perfectly functional and successful in the activity you choose to earn your living.

XIV My First Declaration of Love

The first time I declared my love to a girl I was eight years old, I did it in writing, and I never delivered the letter.

For some reason we Aspies express ourselves much better in writing than orally. The letter had about three pages including the name of the classroom in which I studied my fourth grade, my attendance list number, the name of my teacher (Ramon Milano) and other technical details. In it I declared my sincere and pure love to the Carnival Queen, a very pretty blonde girl who was also studying 4th grade but in classroom "B".

I put the letter in my math book and got up the courage to give it to her at recess at the first opportunity. When I saw the girl I was paralyzed, not only I never gave her the letter but I didn't even say hello to her.

Today I think what paralyzed me was the experience of being constantly excluded as I had been at that young age and that feeling of being a "freak".

It's much easier for us today. Instead of looking for the right moment to look into her eyes, start a conversation, raise my hand and deliver the letter, I just write the letter in my phone and hit "send" or "enter" and then let it happen.

Raising awareness is a very helpful factor, and with this book we are working towards it. You are also raising awareness by reading it. It gradually decreases exclusion, bullying and other traumatic experiences that can cause a child to become paralyzed or an adult to not reach his or her full potential.

Finally the support of the parents, understanding of the siblings, the therapies while the person with asperger is a child, and being an adult the own conscience of the affectations and also the therapy, if it is necessary and the support of the family are factors that disinhibit, increase the self-esteem and can allow a child to smile and deliver a letter or an adult to become what he wants to be, which in my case was always to be truly free and happy, which is what we all want to become.

And that's exactly what I am now.

XV Witness to a Crime

By Iris Rivero, @ReinadMoros

One day I was walking with Luis through Guatire, we were returning from his psychological consultation and we went up to the square through the popular "Subida del Nazareno", on the right hand side there is a naturist shop and when I saw it I remembered that I had to buy some infusions. I've always liked to ask my kids to run errands, not because I'm lazy but because it's important for them to gain skills in communicating with strangers.

I said to him «go up those stairs, they deliver through the window, buy me an envelope of stevia and a green tea please».

I stood on the side of the street supervising my son's shopping, he peeked out and asked for what I had ordered, but suddenly he gasped in amazement and jumped up and down as if he had been given electricity, his scary face scared the hell out of me, but he was clearly in no danger, He turned with a frightened expression in his eyes and said to me in despair: «Mom, get in, come on, here's something you're not gonna like»... Despite the fright and doubt, I decided to wait, while he was being dispatched and given the change. Meanwhile, my aspie was jumping up and down as if trying to see something through the window where he was being dispatched, my curiosity grew, I kept waiting and watching. When the seller handed him the package, he went to meet me with the same anguished expression.

Once we were together again I asked him what was going on, he was still upset and said: «Mom, it's just that in that place, where you sent me, it was written: "Poor Trust is dead – Bad Pay killed him». The literal form in which he perceived that ad made him imagine that he was a witness to the crime of the man called "Poor Trust" and also that the salesman who sent him the infusions was "Bad Pay", who had committed that crime and so with each jump Luis tried to look between the shelves the inert body of the unfortunate Poor Trust.... It was very funny, then when we talked about the situation, I explained to him the meaning of the expression he had read on the wall and he understood it, but at that time he came to believe that I, his own mother, had put him in danger by making him a witness to such a crime... Literality isn't always fun.

Today he asked me to come back to the site to see the poster, now he thinks it's funny too.

XVI Electrified Boots

I know a young couple, she about twenty-six, he about twenty-seven, who have an eight-year-old aspie boy, who, in addition to asperger's syndrome, when he walks, perhaps as part of his motor impairment, puts his feet in, tipping one against the other.

The child's parents, although young and busy, paid due attention to the problem, and since the child's father works in two hospitals, it was not difficult for him to make the corresponding appointment with specialist doctors.

The doctors put the child to walk around, to stop, to sit, to stand, and to walk again. They measured the distance between his ankle and his waist, drew his feet, both of them, on white sheets of paper using the child's feet as a mold; they measured the distance between the toes of both feet when standing, questioned the father and finally gave him the measurements and indications of the orthopedic boots that he had to have made for his son in the place indicated by the doctor.

I saw the boots. They are a kind of black boots with a thick, bulging toe. Inside they have an insole and mould to help make the bridge of the sole of the foot, which is also not formed by the child. But the most remarkable thing about the boots is that at the level of the ankles, on the outside, they have a metal rivet that holds two rubber-lined springs that extend upwards parallel to the legs. The springs end at waist level, where both are attached with another metal rivet to a thick cream-colored strap worn over the pant loops. These powerful springs are not straight but arched outward with enough curvature and size to straighten out a bit as the child grows. As they are arched outwards and not close to the body, they are quite bulky and it is impossible to wear the boots with the springs inside the trousers. The science of this gadget consists in that the metal gouges formed by the springs and the rubbers exert pressure on the child's feet, pushing them outwards and thus making it impossible for one foot to trip over the other, thus correcting the posture.

The child will have to wear the boots all the time, even in the house, for at least five years, probably longer. Each time his boots become too small, the father will take him to the doctor to take the new measurements and make the new boots until he completes the five-year therapy.

The well-meaning, very young parents think they've solved the problem. They don't realize that another one has inadvertently emerged. The little boy who started classes at a new school shortly after wearing his boots for the first time has been facing teasing, prying eyes, laughter and jokes from his classmates because of his walking apparatus. Bullying is a daily occurrence.

Sometimes when we grow up and we're twenty years old, we forget what it's like to be eight and think all these things are nonsense and will soon pass. But it doesn't.

Among the jokes now often played on the child at school is one in which a child approaches him and after grabbing one of the gouges of his boots he shudders, screaming and shaking violently, feigning to be a victim of an electric shock. The children witnesses see the show and burst out laughing. Maybe some people think the joker really got an electric current shock. The little aspie prefers to avoid trouble and says nothing. But it hurts him.

—Do you fall down if you take them off?

—Do they elctrify?

—Can you run?

—Does water pass through that rubber?

—Why were you born this way?

Some questions are sincere, children are indiscreet and want to know. Others are simply to annoy. By now the child has had enough of interrogation, indiscretion and teasing.

Bullying is different from previous years, but just as annoying. This year he did not have to fight, it was not necessary, the bullying has taken a new shade that he did not know. He's no longer the weird, quiet kid, now he's the phenomenon with the boots that give you electric shocks.

The child doesn't talk to anyone. Not even with his parents, not even with his two younger sisters. It's been almost a year since he started wearing the boots and he's about to explode. He feels unable to endure that for another four years. At eight years of age, four years is half a lifetime, waiting half a lifetime is waiting too long. He knows he's not going to make it, that he's going to explode from one moment to the next, and he doesn't know how, but he wouldn't want to because his parents don't deserve it. After all, all they really want is what's best for him, plus his mom is pregnant and needs peace of mind.

The child, who has no friends and not even a therapist to try to tell him what he's feeling, has to go to the doctor for the orthopedic check-up, and since none of the rooms in his house has a door, he locks himself in the bathroom for a long time before going with his father to the hospital. On his knees and eyes closed, as his grandmother taught him, he tells God, the only being with whom he talks, everything that is happening to him. He tells him he can't take it anymore and that he needs help, because he's going to explode. Surely God knows this, but he needs to talk to someone, he needs to express himself, he needs to be listened to, to be helped, and above all to have his feet straightened out without going through that torture. But he finishes praying and nothing happens. Absolutely nothing.

It's been a year since he started wearing the boots. His mother gave birth to a boy, - will he be like him too? It's school vacation time. And they've enrolled him in another school.

How will the new school welcome the phenomenon with the electric shock boots?

The doctor, is the same as the first time. He examined him, did the same tests and measurements

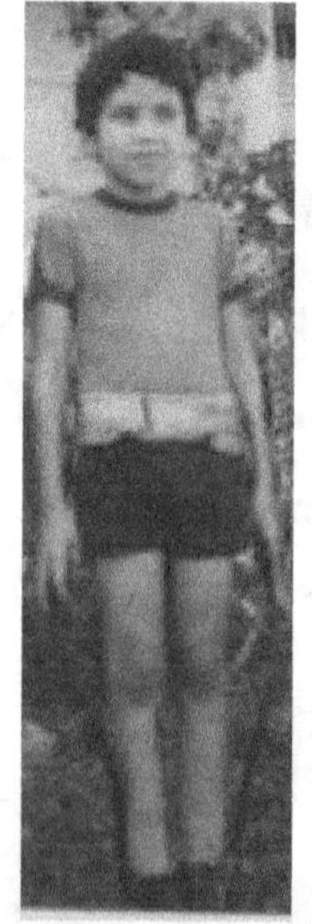

as the previous time and proved to his amazement that the child has his feet straight. He doesn't quite understand how, since it's barely been a year, but it's definite, the child won't need to wear the boots at all anymore.

The father and the doctor are pleasantly surprised, but the child, though unnoticed, is immensely grateful. He knows that God heard him when he prayed in the bathroom that morning and he knows that he will never again be the phenomenon of the boots that give off electric shocks. xxxy

Many years have passed since those days, and I still have my feet straight. Doctor's mistake in the duration of treatment? extraordinarily favorable reaction to orthopedic therapy? mentalization? each one has its explanation to the fact that I only needed one year instead of the five initially indicated by the doctor. But I, although nobody makes fun of me anymore -at least in my presence-, and although I have my feet straight, I don't forget that it wasn't always like that, and that when things were different and I could not talk to anyone, God listened to me, and performed a miracle for me that I will never forget, not only with my feet, but with my faith and trust.

I now believe that no matter what doctors say, if there is love, there is support and there is faith, any diagnosis can positively evolve beyond the logical, scientific and rational expectation of the most learned doctor or therapist.

That's why today I know that as hopeless as your child's diagnosis is, and Asperger's Syndrome is not a hopeless diagnosis, if there are these three things: there is love, there is support and there is faith, your child can surprise you beyond what any doctor or textbook can tell you.

XVII Piano and Speech

The chords of Francis Lai's "Love Story", played with all the passion of young Nelly on her piano, fill the apartment. A ten-year-old boy is alone in his uncle Carlos' room; his mother, younger sisters and aunts flutter around the apartment and the hallway outside. They come and go from place to place talking about work, family and the Christmas holidays. The little boy's sisters are distracted by the noise. The young mother talks to her sisters, the boy's cousin levitates on the piano, the piano sounds and its music seems to penetrate the little boy.

The child has something important to say, which chokes him, which presses on his chest, which distresses him. He approaches his young mother, and tries, but he can't say a word, definitely not one. No one notices his despair and he returns to the uncle's empty room, sits on the bed and closes his eyes. At the age of ten, he is aware that he needs concentration, exercise and faith to do what other children can do spontaneously and naturally, like talking freely for instance. And he thinks about his disability and the desire he has to be able to speak, express himself, communicate as any other child does, except him.

He cousin doesn't stop playing. Music flows from the piano as something almost physical that he can feel. For the girl at the piano only the piano seems to exist and she even seems to be a single unit and since the piano is part of her, she plays it without seeing the keys, rocking slightly back and forth, as if looking at the horizon beyond the wall in front of her.

Little by little the child feels how music permeates the whole environment, you could say that the time has come for the piano to sound just for him, that sitting on the bed with his little eyes closed he asks himself a thousand unanswered questions while letting himself be carried away by the piano.

Suddenly the child is no longer there. Yes, his body is still there, but not him. Those chords penetrate his ears, reach his inner being, and make his soul vibrate. His spirit was elevated by music, and along with the piano chords he now travels without physical limits. His small body is small to his soul freed by music, freed from the disability of his physical mind and the limitations of his body.

He can fly, but most of all he can talk. But not to speak as he does in real life, where for some reason, despite having in his mind perfectly clear the idea of what he wants to say, when he opens his mouth in front of another human being, the right words slip out like water in his hands, tries to fix them like you would fix wooden boards with steel nails to a wall, but he can't. He has not yet discovered the power of writing to fix and order ideas, nor has he developed an alternative technique or strategy for it. The message escapes him irretrievably as always. A thousand words and thoughts are crowded into his head at once, like a whirlwind, about correct intonation, selection of the best words for the case, pauses, possible reactions of the listener, look, judgments, speed of speech, probable interpretations of the listener, type of language... and the speech or talk - however short it may be - becomes a disorganized puzzle impossible to be put together on the spot in front of the interlocutor.

But there he remains with his eyes closed, transported by the piano, in an ecstasy where he can speak fluently, and put together perfectly and coherently with his own voice complete sentences, phrases and stories.

— Yes, don't stop playing cousin, keep going because now I am free, free like your music, to express myself and make myself understood and to be loved and valued - he says to his cousin in his mind.

The words and ideas flow in his head, perfectly clear as the piano chords. But the music stops and the child opens his eyes and returns to reality. That world where music transported him and he could communicate and the listeners paid attention to him and understood him, is an imaginary world. It does not exist.

—The best thing is to escape from home. To run far away and never return to this world I live in. What if I disappear as my words do when I try to talk? After all, my mom already has another male child whom she truly loves. For my mom he is beautiful, he is good and he is worthy of her love. And how can I be worthy of love if I don't even know how to say what I mean? I believe that if I disappear no one will notice, will they? But when will they notice it? And if they do notice it, will they care or will they be relieved? I am leaving the house, so my mom will understand everything I feel, maybe she will look for me, but I don't think so, however if she looks for me it means that she does care about me... Running away is a way of communicating without words.

The piano begins to play again, but the child can no longer cope with his feeling of helplessness and has already made a decision. He must leave his family forever, and make his life. He knows of a boy named Alberto Zapata, who a few years ago escaped from the house where he lived to make his life, and was never heard from again, perhaps he will do well.

The piano sounds, everyone is distracted, the door to the street is open, there is a gate in the middle of the hallway outside that leads to the stairs and the elevator but it is open. He' s already in front of the elevator. He has time to return, no one will ever know about that moment of madness. Or is that not madness but sanity, and madness is living that torture of not being able to express oneself? No, what he is doing is not crazy, on the contrary, it is the only way he has to give a message, to ask, to know:

-Do you love me?

-Do I matter?

-Why can't I talk to anyone at school?

-Do my parents miss me?

-Am I good for anything?

Yes, it really is the only way to ask all those questions without words and say many more things.

He entered the elevator, reached the first floor, and now where will he go? Where will he sleep that night, and the next, and the next?

— Alberto, the big boy that I know and who escaped, knows how to defend himself, but how am I going to survive alone in the world? —Reflect —.

As he walks down the street, he thinks about all these things.

—Will they have noticed that I ran away, will they be relieved, will they be happy, or will my mom come looking for me?

He enters a playground, sits on a bench and tears finally start to flow. He realizes that he is not important to anyone, he is not necessary and surely when they realize it they will be happy for that.

Some children play, it seems they know each other even though they may have met right there, a few moments ago, but they talk to each other as lifelong friends. As he meditates on all these things he sees his mom in the distance walking towards him. She calls him but he feels ashamed and runs away. She runs and calls him with more authority and he, who has always been a very obedient child, or tries to be, does not resist and walks toward her.

Then, in silence and without giving an explanation or saying a word, he hears his mother say:

—Why are you doing this to your dad and me?

—Do you want me to give you away to be raised by your Aunt Nelly?

—Ah?

—Why don't you answer?

—Where were you going

—Are you crazy?

He no longer cries. He can barely stammer a few words between shame and pain. But in his head there are thousands of messages flitting around without knowing how to express them.

But he no longer hears what his mother is saying. The very fact that she went to look for him, is the wordless confirmation that he is important to her. And although there are many things that he still cannot understand or express, that confirmation gives him the right strength necessary to continue hoping and believing that one day he will find the way to free his soul and express what he carries within.

What I like best about this story is that the hope that was born in the child when his mother went to look for him, was not in vain. A few years later he learned to communicate his feelings and ideas in writing, and then to make written drafts before speaking, and so he learned to express himself little by little, more and more naturally, and although at first he thought that no one would ever read what he wrote, or listen to what he had to say, right now he is writing these lines with the certainty that they will be read by many people in the world, including you, dear reader.

XVIII Maribel. The Day I Decided to Speak

By October, the month classes began, I was eleven years and four months old, and had spent my entire life in isolation: isolated from my parents with whom I did not talk, hug, or look into their eyes; isolated from my neighbors who I didn't even say hello to; isolated from my brothers, I only talked to my sister staging fantasy characters taken from my imagination; isolated from my classmates with whom I was never able to communicate because I did not learn the necessary social codes, and because my communication attempts were crashing against a wall of indifference. But now I was eleven years old! and had been promoted to the first year of high school. It was a new stage, I was going to a new institute, I could start from the beginning, pretend that I was normal and that I could communicate and socialize easily, everyone would believe me because they had never seen me before, I would even stand up on a desk and sing a fashionable song, I just had to decide which one, and I would do it in front of everyone, the girls would love me, the boys would admire me. I had everything planned, nothing could go wrong.

The first day of school I was very anxious, there was a familiar face, Rangel and he would surely discover me in front of the others, how could I now pretend in front of him that I was "normal" when he had studied with me for half of my existence -five years- and knew that something was wrong with me?

Rangel would surely tell everyone that I was strange, that I didn't speak and that no one included me, so the children suggested by him would not believe in my performance representing a "normal" child and everything would be a failure. It was my first day of school, my first class, my first hour and things were not going well. I had not considered that possibility in the plan I had drawn up during my school vacations, things were getting complicated, but what I could not imagine was that the worst was about to happen.

The guide teacher, a tall, thin, 23-year-old blonde, wearing heeled sandals and corrective lenses, passed around the list and everyone said "present" and raised their hand, in that while I am pondering the new and unexpected situation looking out the window from my desk and thinking about the strategy I was going to take, I hear that the teacher, Esperanza was her name, says for the second time: "Maribel Cedeño", nobody raises their hand or says "present". Cedeno was not a common last name where I lived, in all my life I had never studied or personally met another person who had my last name, except my cousins and my uncles. Obviously it was me and there was a mistake in the list that was handwritten.

—Maribel Cedeño," repeated my beautiful teacher for the third time.

I had to think and decide quickly: stay quiet as I had always done up to now and pass as non-attendant (or even as not enrolled because maybe it was a mistake in the registration), or I could raise my hand and say loud and clear that it was me but that there was a mistake in the list and it was Manuel, not Maribel. I had never spoken in public, I had never intervened in classes, but I was determined to change, to be different, to remain silent was to remain the same and this was my chance to start changing, there was little I had to say, - come on if you can! -I said to myself.

My heart was beating strongly, the classroom was silent, the leaves of the trees that I saw from the window stopped moving, the teacher waited and took a look among the children, nobody answered, she lowered her face and raised her hand with the pen to put the non-attendance but at that moment in a microsecond I decided to start implementing my plan:

—No matter Rangel, no matter the world, no matter anything, I have to prove to myself that I can speak easily, that I can converse, that I can look at others face to face and speak with skill and naturalness. I can contribute, I can do, I can be. Stop it!. Eleven years of frustrated attempts and occasions where I don't even try to communicate, eleven years are enough, up to here this Manuel arrived, from today I am different and nothing and nobody will be able to prevent it.

The first second after the third time that Professor Esperanza misread my name was not yet over, she had already lowered her face and raised her hand with the pen while taking a breath to read the next name. Just at that moment I broke the silence:

—Present teacher, it's not Maribel, it's Manuel, it's me, it's a mistake in the list.

The teacher saw me with her big green eyes over her glasses and smiled as the entire classroom erupted in laughter.

—Maribeeeeeel ha ha ha ha Maribeeeel — shouted the children. If I had the power to disappear, I would have done it forever at that moment.

It was my first attempt at communication in my "new life" and it was shattered, It was much better to go unnoticed and return to my usual silence, so that no one could see or hear me, But no, it was too late, the whole high school would soon know me as "Maribel", the new kid who started first this year and who is a sissy.

Oh, what a great pain, what fright, what a big failure! How do I explain to them that I am not gay, that my voice is like that because I have not grown up yet and that a mistake in the list is not indicative of my sexuality? I better not talk, how can I avoid being called Maribel, where do I hide so that they don't bother me anymore and make fun of me?

My plans to be normal had failed dramatically, not only because I was now known throughout the school as Maribel —I was always called that name—, the sissy boy who doesn't talk, and who is perfect for ridicule, that was enough, but also most of my new companions were violent, cruel and rude as never before in my short life I had met others. There were very few girls because it was an industrial technical school, which made things even worse because of my clumsiness in doing manual work —carpentry, mechanics and electricity—.

If my parents had known about my disability and had known the necessary strategies, Maybe I could have told them about the difficult situation I was going through and with the necessary support one way or another I would have gotten out of it. But it wasn't, and I was about to begin what was undoubtedly the most difficult year of my life. Fortunately I am one of the rare aspies who believe in God, and this saved me.

God operates in mysterious ways, and does things in His own way. It was necessary for my mental health and even for my physical integrity and safety that I was moved to another school, but I didn't know how to ask for it and my parents didn't know the trouble I was going through, Then a miracle happened although at the time I did not understand it as such: At the end of the academic year I passed all subjects with the minimum grade except mechanics and carpentry which I failed, The difficulties of motor coordination and the low grip strength made it very difficult for me to pass those subjects. My parents then had to make a decision to leave me there and have me repeat the first year with only electricity, mechanics and carpentry or move me to a non-technical high school, where those subjects were not taught and therefore I could study second year.

Without me saying a word, they decided to change my high school to enroll me in second year, and there, in the new high school, I discovered three things:

1— That not all children are cruel and sadistic.

2— That there are people who without one understanding why, even without one deserving it, offer you their friendship and support when you least expect it.

3— That even though I had failed all my life to communicate, it was worth continuing to try because I had so much to say and because if I could make myself understood I could be useful and truly free.

When I understood these three things without knowing it, my life was beginning to change.

XIX Quiet

Quiet I am, O precious little girl of the playground,

Quiet I am

but not for lack of empathy

nor for lack of feeling,

I am not that

but because I cannot articulate words

to express this love that I feel

and that it burns in my heart.

And at recess I finally see you in the distance

And I approach you and your friends with courage

but the words don't come out

I remain quiet, always quiet.

And my ideas are lost

in the deep sea of your brown eyes

in the long and irreverent waterfall of your jet black hair

in the delicious echo of your joyful laughter.

Who will give me, oh precious little girl of the playground

the gift of expressing the things I feel?

as do the other kids

those who do not remain quiet.

You and I would meet when the exit bell rings

and we would walk together to your door

when arriving I would give you a kiss

and I wouldn't keep quiet

I would say "I love you" oh my precious little girl from the playground.

But you see, I'm not like the other kids

I am quiet

and I stand looking at you from afar

daydreaming about breaking one day the chains

that tie me to the silence

and that don't let me tell you

how much I love you!

oh my beautiful little girl from the playground!

But I remain quiet, always quiet.

XX Explosions of anger

A reader asked me this question:

— Hi Manuel, did you have explotions of anger as a child?

My answer:

The Myth:

There is a very common myth that we males with asperger's are aggressive and violent as children, there are some who believe that we even represent a danger to the student community and even to teachers.

How ironic! Because many of us children with asperger's are or were just the most calm and patient and together with other children with other diversities the biggest victims of physical, psychological and verbal violence in schools.

Of course, this crude and cruel lie that we are violent has a basis: when a child with asperger's is bullied to the limit, and the bullying still goes on, the physical aggression continues and the scorn continues, the child can spill over and lash out at the aggressor ignoring the social context and doing so with such vehemence that it can actually frighten others.

It's funny but teachers and classmates don't seem to notice the continuous aggression and harassment we are subjected to as children. No one does anything to make this stop. This crime goes unnoticed, even if it is continuous, well known and daily. On the other hand, when the aspie child explodes, it causes such a commotion that it immediately attracts attention and this is usually the perfect excuse to accuse the aspie child of being violent and aggressive, and it is even an excuse many times for the teaching staff to pressure for the child to be removed or expulsed.

But let's be objective, the child does not exploit because he is aspie, the child exploits because of the excess of martyrdom, because of the psychological and physical fight to which he is submitted to the extreme. But to tell the truth, any child, regardless of his or her neurobiological condition, would explode when subjected to the same pressure and pain: if we take the most "normal" child in the class and subject him to the same martyrdom, he is sure to explode and will most likely do so in a much shorter time than the child with asperger.

There are children with asperger's that are violent and show aggressiveness as part of their affections, of course there are, as well as children with Down or any other condition that for some reason are also aggressive, there are. But aggressiveness and violence is not a common denominator in asperger's or high functioning autism, on the contrary, in a large percentage the explotions of anger occur as I explained, as a natural response to the pressure that generates the harassment and continuous struggle that we are subjected to.

So why the myth that the child with asperger is violent? Because it is easier for the teacher and for society to blame a single child and label him or her as violent, than to correct the real underlying problem which is the intolerance of a sick society that attacks what is different, the cruelty of many children - a reflection of the lack of values received at home - and the indolence of the witnesses. This is very difficult to deal with, as it is also difficult to attack the indifference or even worse, the approval of the child spectators and the teachers who often without tools, or out of fear or laziness, do nothing. This and no other reason is why the child with asperger is blamed, instead of attacking the problem from the root, thus giving rise to the myth that we are violent.

The aspie boy

But I have not yet directly answered the original question my reader asked me:

"Hi Manuel, did you have explotions of anger as a child?"

If we are talking about a tantrum because they didn't buy me an ice cream for example, the answer is NO. This type of behavior is pure and simple manipulation, regardless of whether the child throwing the tantrum is asperger or not. But if we are talking about what was explained in the previous section - THE MYTH - the answer is YES and I can tell you an anecdote that better explains why:

The last time I saw that Aspie boy he was eleven years old, I saw him accidentally in the mirror of his sister Maria Luisa's room, I say "accidentally" because the boy never used to see anyone's eyes, not even himself in the mirror. But I remember that he was pale, small, very thin, somewhat wavy brown hair and dark eyes, given his short stature, his look between tender and elusive, his thinness and his extremely sweet voice for a man was evident that he was incapable of any violence, perhaps not even capable of defending himself. And if you add to that his extremely calm character, it's easy to guess that he was the perfect target for any child who wanted to look smarter, stronger, funnier or more "daring".

What you were unable to guess by looking into that child's eyes for a few minutes, even hours or days, was that this fragile, helpless and perhaps foolish child - because such a quiet child "can't be normal" - was the reaction he might have when dealing with bullying and continuous harassment became unbearable for a human being. But wait a moment. Why do I say that it was impossible to guess a violent reaction in that child, if we know that in reality anyone subjected to extreme pressures can react in the most unsuspected way? Yes, I say anyone. You don't have to be autistic to explode if you are subjected to extreme and continuous pressure and bullying. But the fact is that when teachers and classmates get used to seeing such a passive attitude in some children, they are surprised the first time they see an explosion of anger.

The Bullying

I went to classes on "autopilot" because I didn't believe there was an option to negotiate and ask my parents to change my high school. I even thought that if my parents changed my high school, it wouldn't help either because my bullies would find me on the street and tear me to pieces, in addition, I was sure I would find other bullies at the new high school. But that option of talking to my parents did not exist, not because they did not allow me to talk to them, but because it was impossible for me to talk to anyone about any subject. Although I tried to understand the mechanics of a fluid conversation from a very young age, at that time I only gave short, concrete answers to direct questions.

That's why, with my eleven years and no options, I got up every day at 6:00 in the morning and went on "autopilot" to go to high school. I took every step with anguish, with resignation, even with fear, but I was irremediably approaching the high school. My body advanced resignedly, my feet took firm steps one after the other, without hesitation, but my anguished soul wanted to escape, wanted to shout, wanted to run home and take refuge, but I advanced. One step, another step, another one:

—I wish it were different today, I wish no one would notice that I am there, I wish my notebooks were not hidden from me today, I wish I were invisible.

As I approached the high school, I was mentally telling myself all these useless phrases. I say useless because they always realized I was there, and every day the bullying, the martyrdom, the violence started.

—-Why, why? —I wondered.

At that time, there was no knowledge of asperger, nor were there any diets, therapies or help of any kind, and what I did to lower the pressure was that when I had some free time, or sometimes without it, I used to hide for a few minutes and then come back. The high school was bigger, more ventilated and comfortable than most of the high schools in the city, it had numerous laboratories and workshops, many of which remained empty all morning, it also had a very large field that faced a mountain and a river, from where horses without saddles came down from time to time. Then I, when the bullying and pressure overwhelmed me too much, my self invented therapy was to run away to the mountain or to a dark and closed laboratory without being seen and there, hidden, I would fall on my knees and cry alone pouring out my soul before God.

Usually it worked and I would come down from the mountain -where today there is a neighborhood- or I would come out of the lab quietly, and sure that God was somehow going to help me and that he would perform a miracle in my favor, maybe tomorrow, maybe the day after.

The Miracle

One day, I didn't have time to ask for the miracle, because when I returned from the bathroom where I had gone to pee for a moment during the first hour of English, I found my backpack open and on the floor, my notebooks crumpled and scattered, and I no longer had a desk because Mejias, a funny, white, fat kid, had taken it off to sit himself.

The English teacher had gone out for a moment, the children were excited and they were all talking at the same time. The miracle never happened. I patiently picked up my crumpled and scattered notebooks on the floor, tidied them up a bit and put them calmly in my backpack, while thinking about where I was going to sit now because all the desks were already occupied. When I finished that work I looked up and saw Mejias, who sitting at my desk drew a mocking face for me and did an obscenity with his right hand. I just smiled trying not to make a big deal out of it and Cartaya, Rangel, Orosco and Ayala deprived themselves of laughter celebrating the grace that Mejias had done.

At that moment I was short of breath, I felt that all the air in the classroom was not enough to fill my lungs, nor all the air in the high school, nor the city, nor the whole world. I no longer heard anything, the voices of the children became distant, in my mind Cartaya, Rangel, Orosco and the others disappeared, the whole room and even the world disappeared. I had only one continuous and persistent bully before me, and I felt that his bullying of me, his cruelty and his abuse put even my very existence at risk.

About two years later a political uncle of mine tried to teach me the classic techniques of boxing: the cross punch, the jab, the hook, the trunk movement and the foot dance, but it was useless, I am not good with movements, so that morning as all the other times I did not care about the style, the type of punch, the movements, nor the opinion of others, because for me it was not a question of appearances, nor of style, it was a question of survival. I had before me something that threatened my existence and I had to defend myself, and I did it with all my strength, with all my being.

I cannot describe each of my movements because it was like an explosion in which all my strength and even more, was concentrated in the reduction and annulment of what threatened me, so that I did not read faces, did not hear voices, did not measure limits, dangers, consequences, or social context. I hit him with everything, and after he couldn't get up anymore, I kept hitting him until I had no more strength.

That was a shock at the high school where I was studying for the first time since I had never fought there before, I was " new ". From that day on, everyone was commenting, whispering, looking at me out of the corner of their eye and secreting. The level of direct bullying went down to almost zero, Mejias when he saw me from a distance would return another way and in the room he would sit well away from me. Maybe no one would accept me, I wasn't included but at least I could breathe.

If this is what my kind reader means when he talks about " explosions of anger ", the answer is yes, I did have them, unfortunately more than once. Perhaps, seen out of context at the time, I painted myself as a problem child, violent and aggressive. But today I am sure that the violent ones were others, that aggressiveness is not in a child who defends himself after reaching limits where few would go, but rather it is in a society that turns a blind eye to intolerance and cruelty, and that sees what is different as bad.

That morning when I thought the miracle would never happen, it began to happen. The miracle began for me that day three months before the end of my first year of high school; the miracle continued with the change of school that came at the end of the year. I discovered in the new school that not all children are cruel, since I had my first friends there; and the miracle became concrete many years later with the discovery I made of something called "asperger", it was like discovering myself inside that mirror. This allowed me to understand that it wasn't that something was wrong with me, but that I was a holder of a neurobiological disability so common that thousands of those who read me today have it too: you, your child, one of your patients or someone you love.

God has made me part of this miracle by taking this message around the world to raise awareness among those who consider themselves normal to accept and respect neurobiological diversity, to sensitize parents so they can identify if they have a child with this condition and to prevent children with asperger's today from continuing to drown in solitude until they have explosions of anger.

XXI Swear Words

Since I was a child I have always used more formal language than the average person, well pronounced words, some "fancy" phrases and no swearing - not because I didn't hear them at home - and yes, I feel comfortable, talking like this, like a fish in water. I feel that if I use more colloquial language or popular slang it is simply not me; I call things by their correct name instead of using vulgarities or colloquial expressions like "fucking", "damn" or the like.

I remember when I was twelve years old - I didn't know what asperger was, but I knew that I obviously had something - trying to look "normal" I said a swear word by talking "naturally" to my group of friends -I got three at last-. Everyone laughed out loud and began to repeat the obscenity that I had said trying to imitate my tone or what I know: "What the fuck"…

—"POETIC OBSENITIES" —They shouted and didn't stop laughing.

How could they in just three words identify a different accent or tone? I don't know, but the important thing as I always say is not what happens outside us but what happens inside us.

And I remember that two things happened inside me:

1.- I decided not to try again

2.- I smiled and felt proud to have a "poetic" language - that was the word they used to describe my tone - in which even the swear words sounded like poetry.

I could instead select to become depressed and keep trying to look natural by saying swear words, surely as we aspies are very intelligent I would have learned, I would have managed to be more vulgar than the most vulgar of men. But I really feel very good about my "poetic" language. We can change, yes, but the key is to do it for the better, everything is a matter of choice, even feeling good is a matter of choice because it depends not on what happens outside you, but on what happens inside you.

You choose the best option.

XXII Working in a Group

I was eleven years old, I was the smallest of the group, I realized that my classmates were making a mistake when assembling the circuit assigned by the teacher, the teacher had explained what kind of circuit we had to do, it was one in parallel where with two switches a set of six bulbs were turned on and off indistinctly. I would tell them that they were making a mistake, but none of them would pay attention to me, nor would they turn to me. I felt like the invisible child behind them talking without being heard or looked at, I think I was missing some kind of therapy or something to speak with more power, my voice was quite low and my tone weak and insecureThe minutes passed and my frustration increased, the work had to be in a group and I had been assigned to that group.

I thought: "What a pity! I know how to assemble that circuit, but we're going to deliver it badly because of them. The way they are doing it they will never achieve the goal, one switch will depend on the state of the other and that is not the idea, each switch must have the ability to turn the bulbs on and off independently of the other switch".»

I think the professor noticed my anguish and frustration and even read my thoughts, because he said:

—Cedeño —at that time they called us by our last name at school— Come on, take this and build your circuit by yourself here.

Relieved, I immediately started working alone. The teacher had clearly explained how to assemble the different types of circuit and I also had notes in my notebook, so without wasting time I started my work.

What pride I felt when I finished it. Not only I did it first than my colleagues, who were still stuck arguing and making unsuccessful attempts, but unlike their circuit, the one I set up worked perfectly.

How different it would have been if I had taken a therapy that helped me to express myself, I would have been able to work in a group, teach my classmates and deliver with them the circuit well done How different it would have been if that teacher hadn't realized something was going on with me! How important it is for teachers to be aware of this type of situation! how important early therapy is to our children with asperger's, because without proper therapy many of us can learn some of these things — some of us not— but at what emotional cost! That same teacher referred me to the high school psychologist before the end of the school year, but there was a lot of ignorance at that time and it is not surprising that the psychologist could not identify my asperger, by that time this diagnosis was not known.

This same situation that I experienced with my classmates also happens many times to us adult Aspies. We are forced to work in groups. We know how a task is done, but the rules, the group or the leader says that it is done in a way that we know won't work and we don't know how to express ourselves and we get frustrated because we can't communicate the message correctly or because they don't hear us or we can't convince them.

In adult life this is delicate, because it is important to work in a group and know how to communicate, and although as a child I had a teacher who could suddenly realize what was happening and give me the opportunity to work alone, this does not normally happen in adult life where we have to face leaders many times, to the rules, to the opinion of the majority, and to explain to them sometimes that the way they do things is not the only one that exists, and this many times is not easy and brings as consequence a high price, but I prefer to pay it and to do things as I know how to do them even if I am expelled from the group.

Aspie, don't shut up, when you see that in your group they don't know how to do things right, when you know that everyone is wrong, even if it seems crazy tell them how to do it and where the mistake is. If you have to pay a high price for that, pay it. If you need therapy and help to break the bubble and be heard in the outside world, look for it, but don't keep quiet that life is too short to stop doing all that you could do, achieve and get.

XXIII Women's Shoes

A girl from Costa Rica, whose identity was hidden at her request, asks me a question: "Hello Manuel, greetings. My younger brother is aspie, he is almost sixteen years old and has been presenting a series of attitudes that confuse us a little. Since I was a child he used to wear my shoes. Since I had gone to live far away from my house to study, we thought that maybe what was happening was that he missed me, but in the last few months my mom has discovered that on more than one occasion he put on my clothes including the bra and padding for it. His psychologist says that he does not have a wrong sexual orientation, but then we don't understand. What could be going on in his head? We really feel very confused and don't know how to deal with it. That's why I'm asking for your opinion and advice. Greetings from Costa Rica"».

I answer, as always in my experience:

What you're asking me is quite complex, but it's not related to Asperger's. There are many men who like to dress up as women as a sexual fantasy, many of them are transvestites, homosexuals, bisexuals, etc. Others claim to be heterosexual but have a fetish for wearing women's clothes. Usually fetishes and sexual tendencies appear at very early ages and usually last a lifetime.

In your brother's case it may be either a type of sexual fetish or a manifestation of homosexuality, either one. I don't know the case but the fact that the psychologist told you that he doesn't have "wrong sexual tendencies", doesn't mean anything because for many psychologists there are no wrong sexual tendencies and all are equally acceptable.

Tell the psychologist to expressly tell you whether or not your brother is attracted to the same sex so that you know what to do and what to expect.

I warn you that people with asperger's can have any sexual tendency, there are heterosexual, homosexual, bisexual aspies and all variants and combinations. So you can't assume that your brother is heterosexual just because he has Asperger's Syndrome.

Shoes and women's clothing in general, especially if they have been worn, can have a very powerful sexual energy for many men. This may be due to pheromones or a psychological effect, but the fact is that for many men it can be very stimulating to touch, smell or feel a worn-out female garment. What happens with your brother seems to be different because it's about clean clothes, besides you are his sister and the child doesn't smell it or caress it but puts it on.

The closest experience to your brother I have had was when I was twelve years old. I remember I was alone in my parents' room and I saw Mom's shoe collection. She was by then the most beautiful woman in the world and also, though far away in some ways, the closest one too. Mom was a very coquette woman, she had dozens of high heels of all colors and shades, she looked haughty, imposing, elegant... she really deserved to have the world at her feet. I was so small, insignificant, invisible... maybe by touching her shoes I would feel a little what she was just for a moment at least. I saw them in detail, I felt them, I admired them. How will you feel climbing on those three inches? I felt taller, stranger and with some degree of excitement, but my mom, didn't feel closer, neither did I feel more power, more personality or more energy, besides I didn't like to see myself in women's shoes, it wasn't me.

Possibly it was, in my case something related to the Oedipus complex or something like that, but in your brother's case you're not his mother but his sister and it's not just your shoes but all your clothes, on the other hand it hasn't been once but with a certain regularity, so it's probably not a mere curiosity but a fetish or a trend.

I know that it is not easy to talk about this with him, but it is necessary that with the help of a specialized professional - I recommend an adolescent sexologist - the reason for this behavior and his sexual preference be determined in order to know how to approach the case.

Don't be alarmed, but don't be careless either.

XXIV Good Intentions Are Not Enough

When I was about twelve years old in high school I was sent to do a "typewritten" research paper. At that time we had a briefcase typewriter - the equivalent of a laptop today - I was super excited about the opportunity of using the modern gadget.

I spent the whole day transcribing the original with my right index finger, letter by letter, returning it in the lane that held the paper, correcting it with tipex, and finally taking out and discarding the sheet because it had many corrections.

Late in the evening, and after numerous discarded leaves, my masterpiece was finally ready. I looked at my work proudly, tired, but satisfied and happy, and waited for my mother's arrival to show it to her.

Finally, Mom arrived. I could hardly wait for her to change and get some rest to show her what I had done. When I showed it to her with a shy smile, she gave it a quick glance and without making any comment, she crumpled my masterpiece into her fist, threw it away and said coldly, «Bring me the draft» —(

At that time I spoke very little but I didn't converse, and even less about my feelings, I only used short phrases as an answer if I was asked something), so I didn't say anything, I just obeyed. I watched my mother skillfully and with both hands, without seeing the keyboard, do in about ten minutes what took me all day. Finally I saw the result: the work was beautiful, its margins were perfect, the spacing, without "tipex" or overlapping letters, was impeccable.

But what about my self-esteem? What about my sense of worth? No one asked me. As always, I was alone, struggling with my thoughts, with the information I was receiving from the outside and trying to understand without hurting myself, without feeling more what was obvious to me, but fighting against it.

My mother's intention was for me to deliver a beautiful job, get a good grade, help me, support me; and she did the best she could according to her knowledge and information. But I say to you that GOOD INTENTIONS ARE NOT ENOUGH, you have to look inside the child, inside your patient, or your student, or your child. You have to look inside that person you love and want to help, especially if they are within the spectrum of autistic conditions, and have not yet received the therapies and supports necessary to express themselves and to decipher everything we perceive, because then you will have to make more of an effort to understand what they are feeling.

I'm not going to tell you how I felt, because it doesn't help. But I will tell you what I decided. I could have decided never to play a keyboard again, to understand that I was useless and good for nothing; but instead, in silence as always and without saying a single word but a "thank you" with a shy smile, I decided to be as good or better at "typing" than my mom.

The typewriter had a small manual, which explained the correct way to place the hands on the keyboard, the place where each finger should go, talked about the two rows that are handled with the indexes, which fingers are used to type the space, the position of the back, where to place the look and had exercises with increasing levels of difficulty, which should be done without seeing the keyboard and pressing each key with the right finger and the correct position of both hands.

As a good asperger I practiced alone, in a self-taught way and during days, weeks... months. That manual and the techniques became my main obsession. In a few weeks at the age of twelve and without having gone to a typing course that then abounded, I learned to use the keyboard as the best of the experts.

Today I write like nobody else on my computer or laptop, I write using all my fingers on the keys located for each one, without seeing the keyboard, even without seeing the screen. When I type on my computers I can see the screen or anywhere - as I am doing right now by typing this note on my physical keyboard smartphone - without looking at the keyboard, it is a pleasant and productive experience.

I am telling you this story not to brag that I am a good typist but to say something to the Aspies children and the adults who support them:

TO THE SUPPORTING ADULTS: good intentions are not enough, you have to look inside.

TO CHILDREN and aspie adults: what matters is not what happens but what you decide.

XXV The Aspie Little Prince

I read a short tale in Italian, written by Andrea Steffanoni and published in Spazio Asperger, inspired by the French novel Le Petit Prince by Antoine de Saint-Exupér, and the tragic events in Newtown, Connecticut, United States of America in December 2012.

The tale is about asperger, obsessions, stereotypes, the power of therapists, teachers and friendship. If you want to read the original story you can enter this address in your browser: http://bit.ly/ZdRx9u

I thought it was good to include it in this book, to help dispel the myth that all people with asperger's are equal. Here is my Spanish version of Steffanoni's tale, enjoy it:

On his journey to the planets our Little Prince meets a murderer.

The next planet was called Connecticut and was inhabited by a homicidal psychopath.

«Good morning,» says the Little Prince, «do you live here alone?»

«Yes,» says the murderer, «I killed them all.»

«Why?» asks the Little Prince. «So you will not have company. I used to live alone too, but at least I had a rose on my planet, and now I miss it. You know, I'm very routine»

«Roses don't do anything to you», said the murderer, «but men can be very cruel. They didn't understand me, they always turned their backs on me, were rude to me and isolated me. At school I was bullied. I didn't know how to defend myself, and the teacher wouldn't help me. Neither did my mother help me. One day, my anger exploded and I killed them all. They were not my friends»

«I don't have any friends either. They say I'm different, weird. That I come from another planet. This is true at heart. And I was being bullied too. I like having friends, but, I don't know how to make them... You know, I suffer a little from loneliness.»

«Would you like to try killing someone who has bullied you at school?» asks the killer. «I can lend you a gun, if you want.».

«No, thanks», answers the Little Prince. «If they are rude to me, it hurts, but I prefer to go away and be alone». And after a silence he adds: «I find it hard to understand people».

«¿Why?» asks the murderer.

«Because they don't understand me», answers the Little Prince. «I find it difficult to build relationships with others. Imagining that they may think differently from me. It seems to me that my way of thinking is simple and natural, I think everyone should think like me. But this is not the case.»

«I know what you're talking about», says the killer. «That's why I killed them too».

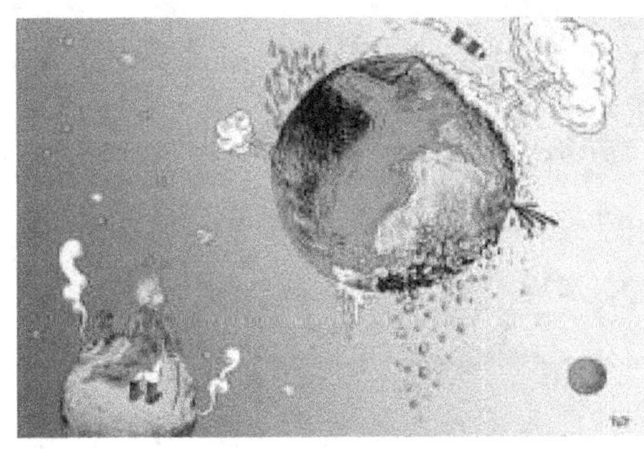

«But I don't want to kill anyone», replied the Little Prince. «I, at most, can throw a tantrum. And when I feel anger I can be very annoying. Sometimes I can't even understand or control my emotions. I need to be

taught how to do it, others say that emotions are easy to understand, but for me it is not like that».

The Little Prince sighed slightly and looked up at the sky.

And after a brief hesitation, he decided to ask,: «Could you teach me about emotions?».

«I don't think so.», says the murderer, «but I can teach you how to use a weapon if you want training in how to use it, do you know how to use it? It's not easy»

The Little Prince replies: «if I had to choose a weapon, I would choose Cupid's Bow, so that I could make some girl fall in love with me.»

And he looked up to the sky again,

«You look so different from the ones I killed» says the killer. «You are sincere, you don't judge me, you are not prejudiced against me. No one has ever been like that with me.»

«I always say what I think» answers the Little Prince, «it comes naturally to me. But sometimes people are offended. They call that 'lack of empathy'. They say that I am not capable of being with others,

that I hurt them with the truth of my sincere words, and they leave me alone. I can't understand it, deep down I'm only sincere».

« You're just plain honest». says the killer. «People are much harder to understand. They think one thing, say another, and maybe even do a third ».

«You know» replies the Little Prince after a brief silence, «even my rose was hidden behind the words. She was so shy and helpless. I should have understood the tenderness behind her tricks. But I was not able to.»

«And now are you capable?» asks the murderer.

«Yes» answers the Little Prince, «I met a she-wolf who taught me. She was determined to tame me. And she did. From her I learned so many things. She was very patient with me. And she did me a lot of good, she helped me so much»

«And then did you kill her?» asks the murderer, thinking deep down that it was a simple she-wolf.

«Of course not, we loved each other. She always understood me. She understood me with her

heart. And she taught me to feel with the heart, not just with logic. She explained to me how to talk to humans, and how to interpret the strange things they say»

And he thought about the she-wolf, who had cried for him, and he thought that maybe, the she-wolf had fallen in love with him a little bit.

And he thought he was truly special to that she-wolf. That it was so beautiful, so nice to be taught. Suddenly he felt sorry for the desperate loneliness of the murderer. He thought that the murderer had also felt loneliness, but instead of finding a she-wolf, he found weapons.

And after a moment he added, «You know, I've met a lot of really strange people»

«Explain to me» says the murderer.

«I met a king, drunks, bluffers, geographers, businessmen. Also with a psychologist. They said strange things about me, that I have a síndrome»

«Really?» says the killer, «that's why I would have killed them. Do you have a syndrome? Which one?"

«Asperger's síndrome»   Says the Little Prince.

«And that's bad?» the murderer asks.

«It depends. If you are loved and supported it is a beautiful thing. It gives you a very pure character, even though you may seem to others a little eccentric or strange. It gives you unusual skills. Like that one about traveling planet after planet, or that one about talking to the rose. But if you are not understood it is hard. You never get to make friends. You are seen as a freak.»

«I think your disability is very beautiful» Says the killer.

The Little Prince was happy. He blushed. He looked at the sky. He took a deep breath. He almost seemed to perceive the perfume of his rose.

«Will you be my friend?» asks the Little Prince.

«Too bad you were so late» says the killer. «If I had found you earlier, maybe I wouldn't have killed anyone. But I can't anymore, it's too late. In fact, it's better that you leave.»

«Why?» says the Little Prince. «It does me good to talk to you»

«Because I will end up killing you. I am a murderer, that is my nature.»

He had a strange, disturbing air. The Little Prince left disappointed.

«People are definitely very, very strange» he said to himself during his trip.

XXVI The Date

Already the first rays of daylight were beginning to fall on the city of Guarenas and the dawn's clarity was timidly beginning to enter through my window. I had been awake for a while, but shame prevented me from getting up to go to my first third-year class in high school.

Just three months ago I was sitting on the floor of that same room playing with toy cars and standing in rows with shoes that turned into toy cars and completed long rows arranged by size, type and color. My room was then the only place in the world where I could express myself freely. As I had not discovered the power of writing as a means of expression, I pretended that it was my toys that spoke and so, through them I expressed myself. I did it in solitude or with one of my sisters who immersed herself with me in my imaginary world that only she and I knew.

What I didn't know that August afternoon when Mariana rang our doorbell and I stopped playing to go after my mom to see who was knocking at the door, was that that would be the last time I would play like a child. But that was because my room did not have a door and the presence of the girl in my house did not allow me the intimacy and solitude that I needed to play.

Wasn't I, at thirteen years and five months old, already too old to play with toy cars and dolls? Perhaps, but those moments when I created imaginary worlds with my toys and escaped to them were the only ones in which I spoke fluently - sometimes too loudly, which often earned me a reprimand, since my mother tried to sleep in the next room.

Those times of solitary play were the only ones in which I felt truly free. I also have to say in my defense that in those years there was no Internet or handheld video games and I was totally incompetent to play ball games due to my clumsiness with the moves, which added to my poor social skills completely eliminated the option to go down and play with my neighbors.

Mariana, who was not named that way but I chose this name to protect her, was a simple nineteen year old peasant girl that my maternal grandmother had recommended to go to work in my house since neither of my two grandmothers could take care of me and my brothers, and my mother had to work.

But now I was there, in my bed, with my little eyes closed and my fists clenched against my heart that was jumping out of that chest of shortness of breath. I really wanted the sun to never rise again. But then the sun came up and my life was never the same again.

Ten hours ago, before I went to sleep Mariana approached me:

—Why don't you talk to me? —She asked. Of course, what she didn't know was that I didn't talk to anyone except the absolute essential. I smiled at her, trying to make her understand that I was open to conversation, but she surprised me with her request:

—But not here or now, —she says, almost whispering and creating a halo of mystery, adding, —I want you to come to my room tonight at twelve o'clock because I have something important to tell you.

I nodded my head and went to sleep at that very moment, 9:00pm as my routine demanded. Instead of falling asleep quickly as I used to at that age, anxiety came over me. On the one hand, the next day I had my first class of third year and on the other hand I had accepted that strange appointment that at the same time terrified and seduced me. All within a few hours. It was too much excitement to drive in one night. I closed my eyes for a moment trying to sort out the ideas, and classify the information:

During the school year that had just ended I had made my first childhood friends: Carlos, Domingo and Humberto who were a very tight-knit

group, and lived on the way to my house about four blocks west on the main street; and Marcelo who was not in the group but had proven to be my friend. The group and I would leave school together, I stayed in my house, and they went on to theirs.

Before arriving at my house we passed by an old abandoned mid-19th century sugar mill on our way in what was once a sugar cane plantation near my house. The mill was made of black cast iron, it was as high as a two-storey house and it was at the end of an aqueduct made of orange bricks cooked and mixed with mud and stones, where many decades ago the water that made it spin no longer passed through. We would get on it and spin it quickly until we were overpowered by the power of the mill and had to jump off it so as not to fall down because of the speed. We ended up panting and happy, laughing at the mischief of not having been knocked down by the mill. I didn't talk much but I enjoyed those moments.

That night I was anxious about the possibility of being assigned to a different course than my friends, and starting again from scratch. Besides I had never had the courage to approach a girl, I seemed to be invisible to them, but inexplicably a woman had approached me and made an appointment with me asking me to come to her room at twelve that same morning to talk to me, within a few hours no more. What if I fell asleep for a long time and lost forever the opportunity to experience what it is like to talk to a woman? Wait a minute, what time is it now? At that moment I woke up startled, without realizing I had fallen asleep, I didn't know if it was hours or minutes, but it seemed like seconds. However, I was sure that it was almost dawn and I had missed my appointment, but I turned on the light of the digital Casio watch that my dad had given me and looked at the time: surprisingly, it was precisely twelve hours, zero minutes, zero seconds. Three hours went by so quickly, and how could I wake up just at the agreed time?

—Maybe this is a sign that I do have to go see what this girl is going to say to me.

Time was flying, I had only blinked and it was already 12:00, soon I had to be in class and I had to sleep, thoughts were galloping in my head, I had fear, curiosity, doubt, desires, panic... But since it was just the time Mariana asked me to go see her and it was likely that never again would a girl make an appointment with me asking me to go talk to her alone, I crept out of my bed and went to Mariana's room. Her room was the first in a long corridor at the end of which was my room. It was necessary to pass through the entrances to the other rooms before reaching hers. Everyone was sleeping, the only room that had a door at that time was my parents' room but it was open and they were sleeping peacefully.

I got to the right room and walked over to her bed. It was dark and I couldn't see well, I stood next to her not knowing what to do but Mariana who seemed to be awake, almost scared me to death when she told me:

—I knew you were coming! But don't just stand there and sit here —and she made space for me.

When I was close enough to see her with the moonlight coming in indirectly through the window, I asked her what she would say.

—I wanted to tell you that I am very afraid and I want you to take care of me, can you do that? —I nodded and sat there, stiff, like a statue, but she insisted:

—Not like that, lie down here next to me and you'll take better care of me, I'm really very scared —I did it, and I lay on her left side, face up and facing the ceiling, stiff as a mummy.

—Can I tuck you in? —she asked, and I said yes, while keeping my cold, rigid posture. She tucked me in with her own sheet and curled up next to me. That was the moment when I first felt the skin of a woman. I am not going to describe everything I felt with the contact of her skin because that is not the purpose of this story, but let's summarize it in that a powerful electric shock and an explosion of hormones completely disinhibited my body and clouded my thinking. There were no longer any words for me, no doubts, no ends, no fear or anything, only the caresses of that young woman that I was experiencing with all my senses, as if my whole life was ending and beginning precisely at that point of time and existence.

Just as I woke up startled and when I looked at the clock and it was just 12:00 am, at that very moment I looked into the doorway, just a second before a shadow appeared on the left edge peeping out and quickly hiding again in the gloom and I heard some returning steps.

The world stopped for me, even though it was dark I know they saw us and everything became small. I let Mariana know what happened, she told me:

—Go away! —she pretended to sleep and I ran to my room and pretended to sleep too. When I left Mariana's room, there was no one around, but I'm sure someone saw us. I couldn't cope with the shame and fear of what would happen at dawn.

And there I was now, my soul empty with shame, facing the wall and fully clothed to the head, with my fists clenched to my chest and my eyes closed wanting it never to dawn. I who tried to be an exemplary son, who read the Bible since I was a child, now failed my brothers, my parents and God.

In my third year of high school I had an irregular schedule with some mornings off and others starting late, so sometimes I was left alone with Mariana at home, as my brothers were in class and my parents were working. She took that opportunity to play along and I took that opportunity to continue enjoying those bursts of pleasure.

That experience was a setback for me. I became more aware of myself, Domingo, Humberto and Carlos, with whom I played in the trapiche, realising that I was distant from them, stopped playing with me. Only Marcelo, the first one who approached me, in spite of my seriousness continued to treat me as if I had not changed and he did so for many more years. Since I no longer spoke through my dolls and toy cars, or played with my sister, I began to communicate in writing the things I felt, and I did so by writing Mariana tormenting letters full of desire, guilt and fear.

I remember that many of the boys who studied with me talked about sex as experts, the truth being that most of them had not yet had any experience, due to their young age, but I, who was younger than them and who was living that relationship with a woman, was not able to say a single word about it.

That kind of beautiful love that, in spite of never having declared it to the girls I fell in love with, made me see the world more beautiful, no longer existed. I didn't feel anything. I lost the desire to make friends, to have a girlfriend, I even lowered my school performance. Sex and those letters, became my only escape to the outside world, my obsession; I no longer played, dreamed, felt, I just let off steam with that mechanical and animal sex, seasoned with guilt, resignation and confusion.

One year we had with that relationship that I don't know the name of, girlfriend? I don't think so, I didn't feel any physical attraction, nor did I want to get married or have a life with her, concubinage? not at all! I was only thirteen years old and was supported by my parents. However that relationship ended a year later in my vacation from third to fourth grade (penultimate year of high school), Mariana had a failure to fulfill her duties, I believe in the schedule, and my mother fired her without a word of warning. Since there were no cell phones in those days and I didn't have a phone in my house, I never heard from her again.

The truth is that I felt relieved, free, and it's not that I didn't like sex, but that I had been living a very overwhelming life for myself, especially because of the guilt that made me feel immersed in love, friendship and dreams. I believe that as the Bible says in Ecclesiastes, everything has its time and its right environment, and it is not profitable to live things out of that time. But that is my experience.

I thought that it was not going to be possible, but finally I felt again and I fell in love like I did before, and just like before I was not able to talk to the girl I longed for, but the important thing for me, is that I felt the love.

Nine years later when I married a girl I fell in love with and met when she was still a minor -I'm two years older than her-, I was still suffering from premature ejaculation conceived in that time of stormy lust, where everything was fast, sinful and mechanical, with the adrenaline rush of a million and the fear of being suddenly discovered by someone who came or passed by the entrance to the room. There were traumas and deviations that lasted for many years and the marks perhaps for a lifetime.

Today in the 21st century it seems normal to start sexual relations at thirteen years of age or younger, I don't know how those children will feel, I'm not in them and I don't know how they will feel if in addition to early sex they have conditions on the autism spectrum, but what I do know is that I lived as a child in the condition that lived that experience in an unsuitable environment and I can say that despite the pleasure, it was not profitable.

Do not let anyone steal the innocence of your little aspie, within your reach do not leave him at the risk of a temptation or pressure that he may not be able to bear, let him live his stages one by one, but above all enter his world and make him feel comfortable talking to you, so you will protect him from others taking advantage of his weaknesses and he will be able to tell you what he lives and feels, knowing also that he does not need to rush into anything because like you, he is worthy of all the love of the world.

XXVII Echolalia

Until the age of fourteen I suffered from mild echolalia. I usually repeated the last sentence I was told, this was almost always done in high school or school, and I guess it was a kind of attempt to start or continue a conversation.

They told me:

—The teacher is not coming today

—The teacher is not coming today —I said

-Tomorrow there are no classes

-Tomorrow there are no classes

One day in her fourth year of high school, a classmate named Jenny called some of our classmates to come see the circus:

—Such a thing," he said, —Yes, such a thing,— I repeated.

Everybody, having been warned, started laughing. At first I didn't understand the joke until the third time it was obvious. Once I became aware of the problem I decided to remove it from me without mercy. And I did it.

If you become aware of one of your afflictions, you can attack it to eliminate or control it, and this at any age including children, you just have to be aware, want to do it and practice. Therefore, if your child is aspie and you detect this or another problem, you can make him/her aware that he/she has this condition and instruct him/her to correct it. If you are the aspie and you are an adult, read a lot about asperger. As you learn, you will be able to identify the different affectations you have, work on those you want to eliminate or change. I assure you that you will achieve many positive changes.

XXVIII Porn Addiction

When I was fourteen years old, a new, middle class, innovative and bold newspaper called "El Diario de Caracas" (the Newspaper on the Beach), had the brilliant idea to increase its sales, to insert on Mondays a supplement of about twenty pages with full color photographs (at that time the newspapers were black and white) taken that same weekend, of beautiful girls swimming in the Venezuelan beaches. Any girl who went to the beach was susceptible to appear on the cover or on any of the pages of the newspaper. The trick triggered sales.

The newspaper kiosks put the Diario de Caracas on display, but instead of putting the front page on display and leaving the insert inside, they put the Diario en la Playa on display and the newspaper behind. I, who had only seen comic strips and family shows on TV, who had never seen a playboy magazine or anything like it, when I first saw the " Diario en la Playa " hanging on the clothesline of a kiosk I was absolutely hooked.

I knew that pornographic magazines existed, but I hadn't seen them, nor was I curious about them, and even if I had wanted to buy one, I couldn't because I was a minor, but anyone could buy the "Diario de Caracas"!

The first times I bought it, maybe the first months I threw it away without reading the body of the newspaper and kept the novel supplement "Diario en la Playa" to look at it calmly in my loneliness.

Although months later I began to read the newspaper to make better use of the investment, collecting and delighting in watching the " Diario en la Playa " became a total obsession for me. My new restricted interest.

Since I did not converse, I did not share my obsession with absolutely anyone, not with my brothers, not with fellow students, not with anyone at all. I looked forward to it every Monday. I saved dozens of those supplements. I ordered them by beach, by date, by the model's degree of beauty (I gave them scores), by type of underwear, etc.

This obsession eventually led to addiction to explicit pornography and compulsive masturbation. Addictions which I had to struggle with for many years even after I was married and well into adulthood.

Note that I am not talking about "regular" masturbation, but about an addiction that is something else; nor am I talking about the beauty of the female body, which is something indisputable and worthy of admiration, I am talking about addiction to pornography. One thing, without realizing it, led to the other.

For people with Asperger's Syndrome or high functioning autism, it is easy to become obsessed with some topic, or issue, and want to know and go deeper into that issue, so these days when it is so easy to get pornography on TV or the internet parents should be careful and ensure that the real and virtual environment where the aspie child develops is the most conducive to him to have good and not bad options to choose as his obsessive interests.

This is very important because obsessions in young people with asperger's are usually strong and last a long time. Any young person can become addicted to pornography but an aspie boy is more at risk because of his predisposition to become obsessed with something and because he does not need to interact with anyone to get pleasure from pornography. Watching pornography and masturbating is an activity that is usually done alone.

In addition to the supervision of the environment where the child and adolescent develop, it is crucial to communicate with him or her and to create a strong bond of friendship and complicity with their parents, this can help prevent the young person with asperger's from feeling lonely and isolated and falling into situations that will be difficult to get out of and can be very expensive.

Don't be careless.

XXIX A Popular Aspie

There was a time in my life when I had many friends.

I was fourteen years old, a junior in high school and the top student in my class. My house was always full of teenagers who came and went for me to explain chemistry, physics and math to them without any interest.

I felt in glory. Everyone admired me, respected me and looked up to me. Even girls from other classes adjusted their shift and schedule to come to my house.

I enjoyed my moment. Also, by explaining to others, I strengthened my knowledge and even understood some new things.

My mom apparently also felt proud of her outstanding and popular son, so much that she decided to throw me a closing party for the school year by inviting all my friends. Now I remember that I kept a record of all the people who visited me, I wrote down in a notebook the names and the number of times they went. I was visited by more than ninety-five percent of my classmates plus some kids from other classes.

My mom gifted me with a state-of-the-art sound system. The ultimate: double cassette deck, equalizer, digital radio tuner and "diamond" turntable needle. As my friends were many and if they came with their girlfriends or boyfriends we would be more than a hundred teenagers in the apartment, she bought a lot of food and snacks. She filled a three-foot-tall keg with ice and beer cans, and once everything was ready and set up, she invited a few of her friends to show off her popular son, and the party began.

No one went, just Mom's friends. The music playing on my new sound system, the snacks served and cooling on the table, the ice melting. No one came.

After thinking about it for several days I understood: the academic year was over, there were no more exams to take and therefore my "friends" no longer had any interest in me.

At that moment, at fourteen years old, I understood that not everyone who appears to be your friend really is, because friendship is shown not when you are up but when you are down. Not always when they smile at you and look for you is because they love you.

Real friends are a very, very rare thing, and if you have asperger's they are a really beautiful thing. The close family and a few people who can be counted on the fingers of one hand are the ones who really love me, and now I value them more.

XXX Letter to a Former Friend

The sound of the Lanco clock that my father had given me, crashing against the wall of the playground, was granulated, solid and metallic. The sound of my companions' laughter was the same as always: humiliating, hurtful, mocking.

But you, who hobnobbed with the populars, who had a girlfriend and friends, and who as if that weren't enough, made a tremendous impression in English and basketball, you didn't celebrate the "grace" of Leal (Pollito), the boy who asked me for the watch to see it and who, without giving me any time, threw it up and kicked it hard before it hit the ground, smashing it against one of the walls of the playground. Instead of celebrating like everyone else, even though you didn't know me, you went as far as the exploded watch, you leaned over, handed it to me and said a few words that I can't remember, but that made me feel that I wasn't alone.

The first thing I thought was that it was a joke of yours. In my mind I saw you pretend to give me the watch and just when I was about to take it, you would throw it to another child as if it were a ball, and this one to another, and this one to another, and so, they would make it impossible for me, "the old man" to get my watch back (or what was left of it), but that did not happen.

I had been nicknamed "the old man" when I was twelve years old, even though you and the other kids were thirteen and fourteen, maybe because regardless of whether the victim was me or someone else, I didn't laugh when a kid was bullied; or maybe it was because I wrote literary compositions that left my Spanish teacher, Carmen Berríos, astonished; but even though I didn't like the nickname, I was relieved with it, because I hadn't suffered physical aggressions, terror, or nicknames that hurt my sexuality as it happened in the high school where I came from, the one where I studied first year of high school and lived the most terrible moments of my life. So the fact that they called me "the old man" was a breakthrough.

But you, you came to me with your watch in your hand and not only called me by my name, but you also showed me that for you I was not the boring old man who doesn't laugh when someone falls down, nor the silly little boy who excelled in chemistry, math and writing, nor the little boy that girls ignored and boys bullied from time to time for pleasure. You made me feel like a person, valued, appreciated, and when no one seemed to care, when I had no idea how to express my feelings and emotions to others, you reached out to me and gave me your friendship unconditionally. And that is worth a lot.

In all my life I have made three close friends: two in my childhood: you and Léner and one in my adolescence: Richard. Of all of them you were the first to approach, but with you it was the same as with Léner, my other childhood friend: after many years and being adults, you decided to break off our friendship with no turning back. What does it matter when you have so many friends? One friend more, one friend less, does not affect anything in that case when you have many friends. But that was not my case. At the time you broke off our friendship you and Richard were the only friends I had and with you I had a closer friendship than with Richard, in fact yours was the deepest friendship I have ever had with anyone and will surely have. How many things we do not live, nonsense of children and boys that are unforgettable. Only to you I told when I fell in love, when I dreamed, when I fought.

As a man I never told you, but it hurt me, that you were no longer there. But how could it not hurt if you were the only one who knew me so well? And how can it not hurt if it was you who held out your hand to me when I thought I would never have a single friend in life? I confess that even today, years after you ended our friendship, I sometimes dream that we are still friends.

But I can understand that your mission in my life has already been fulfilled and I do not reproach you for anything, because the friendship you gave me, you gave it to me with all sincerity, without any interest. You became my friend without even needing me for anything and you came at a time in my life when I needed a friend most, to show me that not all children and people are the same and that I had value and deserved respect.

That year I met you I was able for the first time to successfully socialize with several classmates and we had a good time. Thank you for introducing me to them, but only yours was a true friendship that transcended high school, and then college, and then beyond; they were just classmates I shared with at the time, you taught me how to do it, thank you.

So, no matter what happened next; fifteen years of a true friendship is worth more than a lifetime with hundreds of fake friends, and I will never forget that.

XXXI Jeremiah

I am now an adult and can see and understand things in hindsight. When I was a child, I didn't understand why I was different from other children, and many times I wanted inside to be just like them. But when I was ten years old, I was reading the Bible one day and I came across a boy named Jeremiah in its pages. Jeremiah was different from the other children because he did not know how to speak (Jeremiah 1), he spoke but very few words, he only talked with God in prayer and in his mind, but with the other people and with the other children, he only said short and frugal sentences. He was not like the other children. But one day God told him that he would speak before kings and queens, that he would give speeches before crowds and before children, old men and powerful people. This reading amazed me, because I felt that there was a God in heaven, who knew about me and was capable of doing impossible things even with children like Jeremiah... or like me.

In that same book of Jeremiah, later on I could realize that God's promise was fulfilled, because that child who could not speak became a very recognized speaker, a prophet who spoke with the same ease to children and kings, to ministers or to the people; and his fame transcended even beyond the borders of Israel.

And the story goes that Jeremiah is one day in the house of the village potter (Jeremiah 18) and the craftsman is sitting making clay utensils, all very similar to each other. In that Jeremiah sees that the potter suddenly, after he had made many similar utensils and was making what seemed to be another one, in the middle of the work, kneads the clay again starting from scratch and makes a very different utensil from all the others he had already made, with a different result from what it was supposed to be.

Jeremiah, who was not a potter, because sometimes we judge what we don't know, the first thing he thought was, alas, the potter was wrong, so the pot was not meant to do. That utensil had to be like the others that are there. But God told him in his heart:

—The potter was not wrong Jeremiah, don't you remember when you were a child, the potter did as he wanted, because he wanted to do something different, something more beautiful, something more pure, something different, and I am like that potter Jeremiah, when I love a child in a special way, I do it differently.

I was a child like Jeremiah and today that I am an adult I can tell you with all propriety that God did not make a mistake with your son, you mother who read me; father, God made your son as he wanted, it was not a mistake, he is as he is because God loves him in a special way and wants you to see your son and the world, with the same eyes that Jesus sees them.

God bless the children of all the parents who read to me.

INDEX

If you found this book on amazon please leave your rating and comments.